Open plan organization in the primary school

K. A. P. Rintoul and K. P. C. Thorne

Ward Lock Educational

ISBN 0 7062 3394 8 casebound
     0 7062 3395 6 paperback

First published 1975

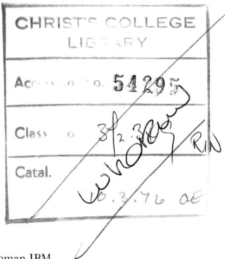
Set in 10 on 11 Press Roman IBM
by Preface Limited, Salisbury and printed by
Robert MacLehose and Company Limited, Glasgow
for Ward Lock Educational
116 Baker Street, London W1M 2BB
Made in England

Contents

Foreword

We, the authors, both serve as general advisers, with a primary specialism, in Derbyshire, and our experience in these posts has contributed to the development of our thinking. However, the views expressed in this book are our own, and do not necessarily reflect the thinking of the Derbyshire authority.

Open plan primary schools are being designed and built throughout the country, often after consultation with teachers, advisers, administrators and architects. The design of the building is intended to help teachers plan their work in accordance with the modern trends in primary education. The integrated day, team teaching, vertical grouping; these are terms used to describe some of the ideas and concepts which have been put forward and considered by primary school teachers. The flexibility of the open plan design allows teachers to experiment and innovate with these and other concepts. Children may be grouped in different ways and there is opportunity for varied activities to be pursued.

We base our thesis on the fact that all children are individuals and have different needs which must be met. Similarly, we recognize that our readers will have different requirements. Some may discover new ideas within this book, others may find confirmation of beliefs already held, whilst others may consider it controversial. We hope that each reader will find something interesting and of value in it.

We wish to thank the following who have listened to our theories and discussed them with us:

Miss R. G. Stapleton, Headmistress — Ilkeston Larklands Infants' School
Mr D. C. Cheeseman, Headmaster — New Whittington Primary School, Chesterfield
Mrs D. Clayton, Headmistress — Sandiacre Ladycross Infants' School
Mr R. M. Gough, Headmaster — Ilkeston Chaucer Junior School
Mr P. T. Godfrey, Headmaster — Matlock Bath Holy Trinity J. M and I. School
Mr F. I. Knight — Chief Adviser, Derbyshire

The teachers described in Chapter 3 are imaginary people. Any resemblance to people of the same names is entirely fortuitous. Similarly, none of the plans used is identical with existing buildings so far as we know. In fact there is no school exactly like any of those described in this book. Rather, we have collected impressions of the ways schools are organized and have generalized about some of the methods used.

Much of what is written in this book is appropriate to any primary school. We have tried to show how the open plan building can provide an ideal situation in which to put into effect the best primary school practice.

K. A. P. Rintoul
K. P. C. Thorne

1 Origins

As recently as the early 1950s there were still primary school classrooms with galleries. Figure 1 shows a classroom in a school built by the London School Board in 1873, and generations of children sat in the tiered rows. The floor in this particular room was not levelled until 1952.

Figure 1

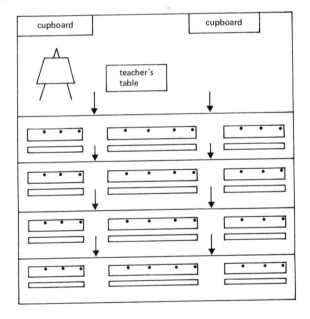

The original galleries in nineteenth-century elementary schoolrooms were like miniature lecture theatres, and the 'object lessons' taught by the teachers to their rows of pupils were often a skilful mixture of lecturing and questioning. Galleries were an essential feature of the large elementary schoolrooms which housed all the pupils in the one large room. Later in the century, the supply of teachers improved and separate rooms for the assistants and their classes of children were built. But the teachers had been trained to give their 'gallery lessons' and even the smallest new classroom had its gallery where children sat and worked. Such classrooms set the norm for decades of teaching in elementary schools. The children faced the teacher, they worked under his direction and they listened to his instruction. They paid attention to his blackboard drawings and notes and often they spent long periods copying sentences and sums from the board. The day was divided into class lesson periods and the competence of teachers was judged by their ability to hold the attention of all the pupils. Indeed, the 'payment by results' system encouraged teachers to ignore the individuality of pupils and to bring them all to the required 'standard' for the inspector's annual examination.

Most classrooms had lost their galleries by the middle of the twentieth century, and children were seated in rows of desks on a level floor (Figure 2). Indeed, children still sit in rows in most secondary schools and in some primary schools today. In this organization the teacher remains mainly an instructor, working from the front of the room and teaching usually by class lessons to which, hopefully, all the children listen.

Figure 2

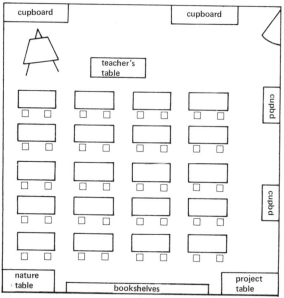

Even the most gifted teacher must find it difficult to hold the attention of all the pupils with their wide range of abilities. To help the teachers, classes came to be streamed according to the abilities of the children so that the groups were, in theory, more homogeneous. But even a streamed class contained children of differing abilities and attainments. With forty children in a junior class, the teacher would be tempted to teach to the class's average. He might easily resort to 'mass teaching' of the whole class so that the highfliers were held back, or the slower learners neglected. The many teachers who cared for the slower pupils could only too easily go at too slow a pace for the others. Indeed, the regimented rows of a traditional classroom made it difficult for a teacher to treat his pupils as individuals, and the move to the 'open plan' schools has been a gradual change to a system which allows for every child to make his own maximum progress.

Many innovations were coming into the primary schools during the middle decades of this century. Dewey's ideas about projects, where groups of children tackled a problem together, led to an integration of some subjects, and classrooms often had their 'project' or 'topic' table where a piece of work was displayed. A 'nature table' too was seen in many classrooms, for the nineteenth-century pioneers of nature study had influenced teachers to believe that the world outside the school could be of educative value within the classroom.

Most primary school teachers have abandoned the system where children sit in rows. Recognizing the differing needs and abilities of individual children, many teachers now group their children by ability in blocks of four, six or eight. The furniture arrangement in Figure 3 shows what is probably the most common form of classroom organization now seen in primary schools. In fact, this diagram shows an extremely inefficient form of classroom organization. It is a sensible enough arrangement when

Figure 3

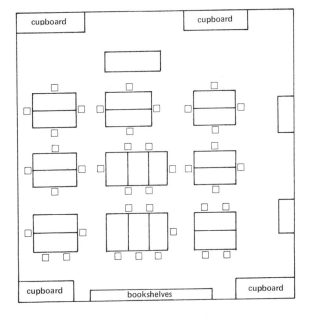

children are seated in ability groups and working on graded tasks and assignments. But the teacher is placed in a position where she expects to receive the attention of all her pupils during a class lesson. This is not easy for children seated with their backs to the teacher! There is also a considerable waste of valuable classroom space.

If this form of grouping the children is adopted, teaching methods must change significantly. The teacher will have to place herself more unobtrusively and, if possible, release more room for the children. She will have to abandon class teaching (e.g. 'chalk and talk') as the main method and she will have to explore instead techniques of group organization. In short, what is needed is a classroom that will provide every possible square foot of space, and yet allow for the variety of teaching and learning situations that will take place during the course of the day. Much of the work will be tackled by the children in groups; at other times children will be pursuing their own individual learning: occasionally during the day, the teacher will wish to teach the whole class together.

In Figure 4 the position of the teacher's desk is significant. It shows that the teacher no longer dominates the room — instead she has attempted to provide more a workshop than a classroom in the traditional sense. The teacher's role is to encourage the children to learn ('learning centred' education is more meaningful in this context than 'child centred' education), and one of her essential skills is to prepare resources and assignments that will keep all the children working at full stretch to the limit of their abilities.

Figure 4

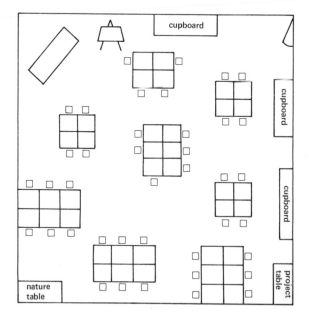

The main difficulty in this layout of furniture and space is that the teacher will find it difficult to give a lesson to the whole class when the need arises. She may find it more convenient to move back some blocks of desks and have the children sit in an arc around her, on chairs or on the floor. With a classroom organized as in Figure 4, the teacher will need to have a flexible timetable. Occasionally in junior schools there will be times when all the children will study the same thing at the same time. This will happen less often with younger children. The timetable will have to be broken down into more flexible and probably larger units. Indeed, the names of some familiar subjects may well disappear altogether from the timetable, for their learning content will be covered through integrated work which is not circumscribed by time limits.

The change from a classroom like that shown in Figure 2 (straight rows) to that in Figure 4 should be attempted by teachers slowly and cautiously. The blocking of desks and the grouping of children could be tackled in stages, and a teacher would probably wish to make several experiments before arriving at the most satisfactory layout. Simple classroom plans could be drawn and rectangular shapes representing furniture to scale could be moved about on the plan until the most spacious and satisfactory layout is arrived at.

In Figure 5 the same junior classroom which once contained a gallery is adapted to become what is probably the ultimate for this box shape.

Only a few children can sit at any one time at the blocks of desks or in the bays, for many of the chairs are stacked out of the way. The idea of children standing for some of their work need cause no surprise to teachers who have observed children carefully. Indeed, much primary school learning need not be done at a desk or table, and new purpose-built open plan schools rarely contain seating accommodation for more than about 70 per cent of the children at any one time.

In this classroom 'integrated learning' is taking place. For example, instead of the weekly art lesson, there will be opportunities for some of the children to work at their art or craft throughout the day. Similarly, mathematics, science, language and other subjects will be pursued by individuals and groups at their own pace. This approach throws great responsibility upon the teacher. Standards of work should not be allowed to deteriorate and careful records must be kept so that every child is kept at full stretch. It is often said that some children in such a classroom will waste their time or take to work which is too easy for them and gives them less trouble. Certainly, these methods will only work if there is a thorough organization of space and equipment. Storage must be carefully considered and provided where it is most effective, and the display of the equipment and of the children's work is also important.

Where a teacher is dedicated to this type of teaching and is able to organize it efficiently, then standards can be very high indeed. The 'Hawthorn effect' comes in here — a teacher who wants to make a method or a medium work (i.t.a. for example) will succeed in doing so. A teacher

Figure 5

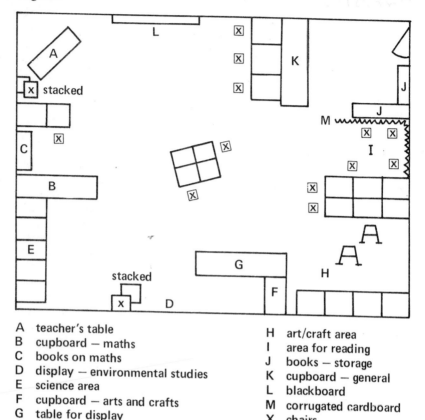

A   teacher's table
B   cupboard — maths
C   books on maths
D   display — environmental studies
E   science area
F   cupboard — arts and crafts
G   table for display

H   art/craft area
I   area for reading
J   books — storage
K   cupboard — general
L   blackboard
M   corrugated cardboard
X   chairs

This room seems to be deficient — sink? books? plants? pets? t v ? radio?

who is resistant from the beginning will find difficulties where none need exist if attention were paid in the first place to thorough organization. One of the teacher's first objectives is to train the children to run the classroom themselves: they must know where things are kept and learn to help themselves to materials sensibly; they must be trained to put things away and to be tidy and responsible; they must present work which they feel is worthy of themselves and be trained not to be content with second-best. Teachers who organize classrooms such as this one will often claim that after a few weeks the children will take over the running of their room themselves. Indeed, the authors have often noticed that children who have been used to this kind of learning from the earliest years in school will behave responsibly and sensibly later in the junior school. But older children coming to this kind of situation for the first time may well be at a loss, feel insecure and possibly behave badly. Therefore, it must be repeated that this kind of teaching cannot be suddenly introduced overnight, as it were. A new headteacher taking over a 'formal' school must make long-term plans for a change to the new methods, and not expect teachers to be easily converted to them, especially if they have had many years of teaching all the children together to a tight timetable.

Of course, there will still be times when the teacher wishes to have the attention of all the children at one time. This may be in order to enjoy a story together, or to discuss a piece of work that has been done or is soon to be pursued. Many teachers want this 'together time' with the children at the beginning of morning and afternoon sessions, and at the end of the school day when the next day's work can be discussed and prepared together. For these occasions, the teacher will have to organize a quick, reasonably quiet procedure so that chairs can be taken from stacks and placed in a group around the teacher. Perhaps blocks of desks will have to be moved out of the way. Many teachers will not require this; the children can simply sit on the floor around the teacher. In this way an intimate atmosphere for story-telling or for discussion can be created. A carpeted space in a corner of the room would be ideal for this 'together time'.

A possible danger with this kind of organization may be that certain aspects of the curriculum will be neglected. Without a timetable to guide her a teacher may find that for too long some children have done no work in science, say, or in history or in some other subject. It is essential that a balance is maintained. The child's intellectual development must be nourished in every possible way. So must his aesthetic, social, physical and moral development, and every school, new or old, has the fundamental duty to encourage the all-round development of the whole child. The teacher's recording system of work tackled and progress achieved becomes even more important when timetables no longer exist in sufficient detail to ensure a balanced curriculum.

The methods used in a classroom such as that shown in Figure 5 were the origin of the so-called 'open plan' schools in which individual and small group learning can take place. The main concepts involved are repeated:

1   The organization of classroom spaces so that children can learn as individuals and in small groups for some of the time.
2   The integration of subjects so that different activities may be going on at the same time.

These ideas influenced the design of classrooms after the war. The class boxes were often larger than those of the School Board schools (certainly so in a 'good' year, i.e. when the Government's cost limits matched builders' tenders). The new, airy classrooms of the 1950s frequently had

13

the equipment that the old schools were deprived of. Sinks, display space, good storage facilities, sockets for radio and TV, carpeted areas: all these became regular features of new schools and allowed teachers much more scope for using the new methods. Figures 6 and 7 show two typical post-war classrooms which have the amenities for 'learning centred' education.

Figure 6   A junior classroom

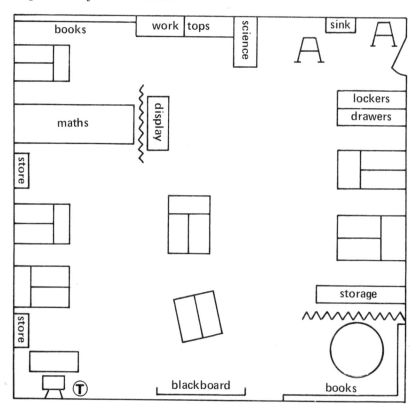

The integrated day
It has been emphasized that a sudden change from the traditional situation to an integrated approach will be unlikely to succeed. On the other hand, many teachers reading this book may be doing so because they are faced with a move to a new school, either because the old building is being

Figure 7 An infant classroom

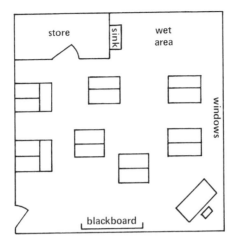

replaced under the nation's drive to improve primary education, or because they are changing to another appointment. These teachers need not be mystified by the expression 'integrated day': like the term 'open plan' itself, we have an instance of educationists' jargon, of a label which on examination is not very meaningful. Few if any 'open plan' schools exist in the country if, by this term, is meant a school which is completely open within its four exterior walls. A better term for the new schools would be 'flexible' or even 'maximum opportunity' schools. The term 'integrated day' is another instance when an educationists' label is misunderstood by the public and by some teachers. Indeed, the term itself has no precise meaning. Moran (1971) identified about five major types of an integrated day used among 181 primary school teachers. The five types are:

1 Numerous activities occurring in the same class at the same time, e.g. language, mathematics, art. The children work at different activities, but they are directed by the teacher; the choice is not made by the children.

Alternatively, children work at different tasks within the same subject activity, e.g. all are engaged in mathematics but at varying levels of difficulty.

At specified times, or at the direction of the teacher, the groups of children exchange activities. This system is sometimes called a 'rotating or circulatory environment'.

15

2 Tasks, assignments or jobs are given to the children who are allowed to decide for themselves when, and in what order, they are tackled. The assignments may be given by work cards, or verbally, or listed on the blackboard.

The time allowed for the completion of the assignment varies from one, two or three days, to a week or even a fortnight. Assignments give the children some control over the order in which activities are to be tackled, but the degree of control differs according to the assignment system being used.

Recording children's work, and maintaining a balance between the various areas of knowledge causes some concern — the system demands a teacher's organizational expertise.

3 Directed work by the teacher during the morning (usually the 3 Rs), followed by some freedom of choice of work by the children during the afternoon ('skills and frills'?).

This 'integrated half-day' stresses the importance of basic skills which are learned separately from the rest of the curriculum. Many opportunities can be lost when basic subjects are divorced from other activities; indeed, many teachers help children to succeed in the basic subjects by using opportunities that arise in other activities.

4 The teacher organizes various activities or 'structured situations' around the room or the school, and the children are allowed to choose their activity. In some cases the children are free to work around the school, until drawn together for collective time.

The teacher may withdraw children for guidance and help with work in the 3 Rs.

5 Children choose their activity on some occasions, perhaps for two days or a week, or the occasional week in a term, or for the odd afternoon (Friday!). This type may be used to introduce newer methods, and may be used alongside more formal approaches. For teachers new to integrated teaching, this system of combining subjects for perhaps one afternoon a week in the first instance may be the best way of moving towards the new methods (see below).

When teachers wish to change to one or other of these integrated approaches, or indeed to their own version, which may come under none of Moran's five categories, they would be well advised to change gradually. The following stages can be recommended as having been used successfully by many teachers when they were preparing for their new replacement schools:

1 Within a tight timetable, and with all the pupils doing the same thing at the same time, the teacher could organize groups working at different levels of the subject, which could be tried for one or two periods a week at first. For example, if the work is on division of number in the mathematics syllabus, then children can be given

assignment cards prepared by the teacher for different stages of the process. Quicker groups of children can be given harder cards to work. Later the groups may be able to tackle different mathematical processes, according to the children's abilities and attainment.

2 Again, for one or two periods a week, the groups could be given assignments in different subject areas, e.g. mathematics, writing, history topic etc.

3 As 2, but without a time limit. Children are permitted to continue their work and then go on to another subject area. At this stage the 'open plan' classroom (Figure 5) will be required.

4 Still within groups, children are given set tasks to do within a half-day: later, within a whole day, or even a week. Gradually, *within* the group more choice and freedom is given to individual children. The teacher sets the targets, and insists on the jobs that must be done. This stage cannot be reached unless there is adequate preparation and discussion with the children. At times the children will be brought together, and again the layout of the classroom will have to be carefully thought out. A quick and effective system of keeping records is essential.

Many teachers within the formal walls of a box classroom would find an integrated day reasonably easy to achieve if it were approached by these, or similar, stages. Indeed many teachers who consider themselves as 'formal' or 'traditional' are already half-way towards the integrated day. To complete the metamorphosis the classroom layout must be worked out, and perhaps some of the diagrams already seen will be of some help.

The development of cooperative teaching

In some old schools it may be possible for two teachers who wish to do so to open a dividing partition. Some of these partly-glazed partitions were originally erected in the old schoolrooms when assistant teachers were first appointed to the school and smaller rooms were formed to break up the large open space. (This is not to say that the old Victorian schoolrooms were 'open plan' in the modern sense: there is no relationship between the methods of the regimented schoolrooms and today's flexible and integrated arrangements of space.)

There may be many difficulties when partitions are pulled back, as shown in Figure 8. Often the accoustics are bad in schools with high ceilings; sometimes the storage is hopelessly inadequate. Nevertheless, many teachers organize a double unit with two of them working together with the two full classes (i.e. up to eighty children).

The arrangement of the makeshift unit in the diagram is self-explanatory. But it is worth noting that many of these older schools have wide corridors which can provide valuable space for some of the more noisy activities. It is also apparent that there is only the mathematics area to be shared by both classes — this can present a considerable saving on the

Figure 8

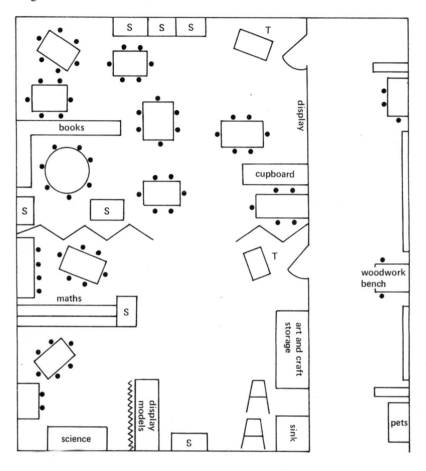

school allowance. Indeed, the sharing of resources is one of the main benefits of cooperative teaching.

Another benefit is the expertise which individual teachers can give to the school. The curriculum of primary education has been developing rapidly over the last few years: the 'new' mathematics, science, French, new reading programmes and so on all demand expertise from the teachers. It is becoming increasingly difficult for any teacher to remain an expert in every aspect of the curriculum, and two teachers may be able to pool their special interests for the benefit of each other and the children. This is not an argument for specialist teaching in the primary schools.

Rather, each teacher has a special expertise which she will share with her colleague. She may be the unit's adviser on language and the teaching of reading, for example; or she may be able to develop the unit's work in mathematics. Her advisory work will include the organization of the specific area to be used by the two classes, the ordering of books and equipment, the passing on of her knowledge to her colleagues, and the advising of her headteacher about the innovations in the teaching of the subject area and the way the whole school staff could be thinking for future curriculum development.

As with the classroom plans previously discussed, the basic practical problems of storage, display and day-to-day organization must be considered. Tidiness is important, and the standards in this – as in other things – can be valuable for the children's education. Records must be carefully kept by the teachers; they may devise simple systems which ensure that every child is working to his potential. Each teacher must, of course, remain the class teacher for her 'own' children, giving them the security and the recognized adult to whom they go for most things. Gradually, the children will learn that another adult is available for some things during the course of the day. Ideally, a third adult – an ancillary worker perhaps, or a student – could also be available in the unit to look after certain aspects of the children's activities.

In a small school the two units shown in Figure 8 would contain children of at least two years' age range. These would be a form of family or vertical grouping which has some educational advantages. In the purpose-built new schools, a primary school is often designed in blocks which house infants, lower juniors and upper juniors, and in each block there will be family grouping, five to seven years, seven to eight and nine to ten.

The makeshift two-teacher unit spilling out into a corridor, and with all the children sharing spaces, became a model for some of the new purpose-built 'open plan' schools. Many local authorities now have schools which extend the idea of two teachers cooperating in their work with children.

The unit shown in Figure 9 has two 'class bases' and a shared activity area. It is 'open plan' in the sense that the teaching boxes need not confine the development of the children's work. Basically, wasteful corridor space has become valuable 'activity' space where children can work at arts and crafts or at other activities where a sink and special storage can be available.

The two teachers will have to work together and decide how to make the best use of the shared area. Also, they will have to work out groupings of children and to organize the sharing of equipment and materials. A third adult, who need not be a qualified teacher, could provide an invaluable pair of hands in the shared space, although her role will be very different from that of a qualified teacher.

Many teachers, forced into one of these units by the closing of their old

Figure 9

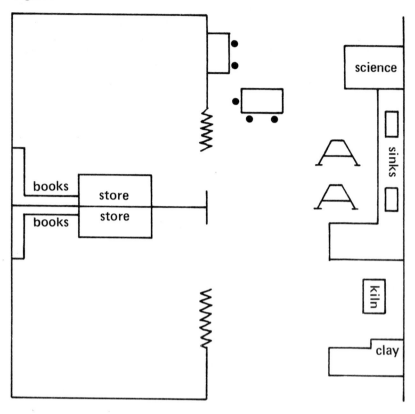

school, would be tempted to close the sliding door on the class base, and even ignore their colleague in the unit. This could be unhappy for the general work of the school, and somehow the headteacher would have to seek a compromise whereby the teacher could retain her independence while still permitting a cooperative spirit to emerge gradually. It goes without saying that the two teachers in the unit should get on well together: compatability is essential if team work is to succeed, and again, the headteacher must take this into consideration. Ideally, the two teachers should get on so well together that they discuss their work enthusiastically, and spur each other on to make the work more interesting and rewarding for the children.

For many teachers the design of this unit is too constricting. The class bases are too isolated for specialist work areas to be planned. In many Authorities the two-teacher units have been made more open and flexible.

There has also been a move to larger units with three or more teachers and their children sharing the spaces. A two-teacher unit can be fairly easy to organize, provided that neither teacher isolates herself in a class base. The problems are much more complex when a three-teacher unit is in operation. Later chapters discuss the problems of larger units where cooperative teaching has to become more structured without losing the flexibility that the schools were built to provide.

References
MORAN, P. E. (1971) *Educational Research* Vol. 14, No. 1, November

2 A flexible way of working

In this infant school designed in a traditional manner and erected about 1964, classrooms were built in units of three with shared lavatory and cloakroom facilities (Figure 10 see page 23). The classrooms were designed to accommodate forty children and the unit is staffed by three qualified teachers and a full-time ancillary helper. Each unit has a caretaker's store which holds a sink, and some storage space. Each classroom has a walk-in store room, trough sink, narrow partition walls (5' 6" high) to create 'bays', and an external door leading on to grass and paved areas. This door provides an alternative exit in case of fire, but also allows classroom activities to overflow outside in fine weather. In addition, each unit has access to the hall and a double-door exit to pavements and grassed areas, and to the playground. Each classroom is approximately the same size (i.e. 740 sq. ft.) and has much the same provision. Classroom 2 is arranged according to Figure 11 (see page 24). There is seating for up to forty pupils, but because the tables are arranged round the walls quite a large amount of space is left centrally for children to move about freely as they engage in various activities. The room is arranged in work areas.

Children keep their own belongings and work books in the trays provided under the far end of the worktop; there are forty of these trays. Maths apparatus is kept in the cupboard located under the central portion of worktop and a variety of art and craft material is stored on open shelves under the remaining third of the worktop. These materials are kept in large cardboard containers obtained from local shops, covered with patterned Fablon so that they are strengthened and look attractive, and clearly labelled with the names of the materials they contain. Children are thus able to find the materials they want, for themselves, and know where to replace any unused bits and pieces. Various kinds and sizes of paper are placed on a table close to the easels.

The two free-standing cupboards, about 4' 6" in height and 5' in length, are arranged so that they open into the centre of the room. In one, table-toys, jigsaws and the like are to be found, and in the other reading schemes and apparatus for language learning and development are stored in such a way that children can collect the book or piece of apparatus they

Figure 10   Plan of a three-class unit in a traditional building

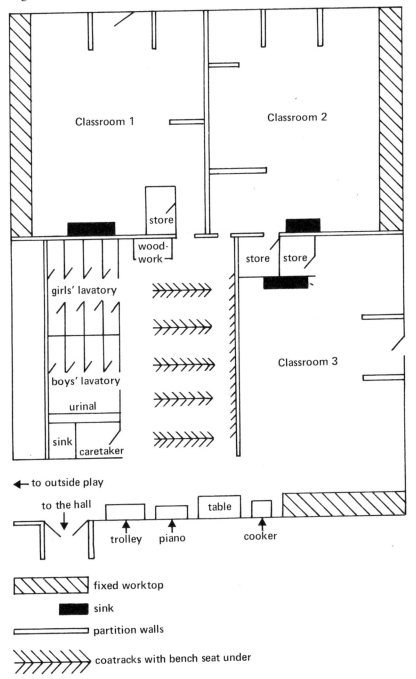

Classroom 1

Classroom 2

store

wood-
work

girls' lavatory

store   store

boys' lavatory

urinal

Classroom 3

sink

caretaker

← to outside play

to the hall

table

trolley   piano   cooker

▨▨▨▨   fixed worktop

■■   sink

▭▭   partition walls

≫≫≫≫≫   coatracks with bench seat under

23

Figure 11

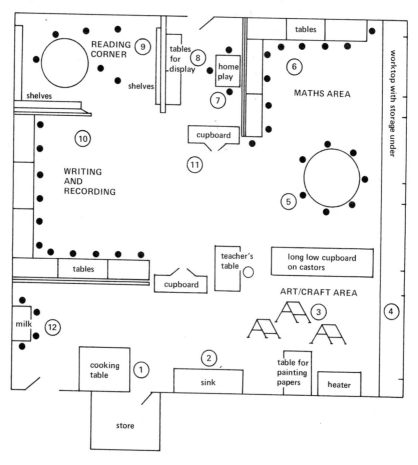

need and return it to the appropriate place. To help the children replace books and items of equipment various coding systems are used. A colour-coding system indicates which reading books are of the same level of difficulty, whilst apparatus consisting of small pieces is marked on the reverse side with symbols to facilitate sorting. The backs of the cupboards are used for display purposes.

The long low cupboard, about 2′ 6″ tall, which opens into the art/craft area contains all sorts of materials, cottons, silks, braids, sequins etc, for collage work and the Formica top forms a useful working surface.

The large walk-in store holds not only the reserve supply of stationery and materials but also large pieces of apparatus and expensive items of equipment: this can be locked overnight. During the day, however, children have access to the store and can help themselves to the apparatus and equipment as they need it so long as they return it to the proper place. The sink, about 3' long and 1' wide, serves a number of purposes. It is easily accessible for washing up cooking utensils, and also provides water for art/craft activities. A rack placed over the sink holds various measures for capacity work.

There are display (pinboard) panels attached to the partition walls and to the walls over the heater, in the maths area and the writing/recording area. Windows are situated in the reading corner and along the full length of the wall over the fixed worktop.

The children come into the classroom first thing in the morning, and begin to work immediately. Some may have tasks to complete from the day before. Others may have planned a new activity and so collect the materials they need and set to work in the appropriate area. Some may have writing to do, whilst one or two may wish to find information from a book, or complete a story begun the day before. Children who are used to this way of working can plan their own work and do not need to wait for instructions from the teacher, but move from area to area, and from activity to activity as the need arises. If one watches carefully one sees that this movement is not random but that the children are following patterns of learning, and that they progress logically from one situation to another. If, however, a child wishes to move into a particular area and there is not a place for him immediately, he learns to accept the situation, moves to another area and returns later to do the task he had intended doing. Thus a child may find something which interests him in a display, go to the book corner to find out some information, move into the maths area to do some related mathematics and finally make a painting or model of his own. Movement about the room is purposeful and may be dictated either by the personal interests of the child or be planned and initiated by the teacher.

This flexible way of working allows for a variety of groupings to occur throughout the day. For particular teaching situations the teacher may group children according to ability or stages of development. Children may group themselves with friends for some activities, or may choose to work with children who share common interests. Sometimes the teacher deliberately groups children who are incompatible for short periods in order to foster better relationships through working together. Thus over a period a child may find himself in one group for flash card work, in a different group working in some mathematical pursuit, with a group of his friends in the home play area, and with another group at a later stage, working on a model of common interest. The groups also vary in size and duration. Some are deliberately planned by the teacher – others just happen.

The teacher moves around the classroom, helping, encouraging and talking about what the children are doing. She asks questions and makes suggestions. She has planned her day and knows which children she needs to be involved with for direct teaching purposes. She knows which children she needs to hear read individually and will call them to her for that purpose at intervals throughout the day. She will know whose work she needs to check, where she needs to introduce new material, or where she needs to intervene to ensure that work develops. She will also draw the class together as a whole from time to time for stories, discussion, physical education, singing together, or the introduction of new topics. All the time she will be observing the children, seeing where they succeed and why they fail at certain things, and through this close observation is able to provide for the needs of each individual.

During the day children are to be found scattered throughout the room engaged on different activities. For instance, there might be four or five cooking. Over the cooking table (see 1 on the classroom plan) a list of instructions indicates that before starting to cook, each child must have washed his hands and put on an apron. There is also a selection of recipes. A range of ingredients in clearly labelled containers and the necessary tools are stored in a low cupboard beneath the table. The children, under the supervision of the ancillary helper, weigh out the ingredients, mix them, put them into baking tins and take them out to the cooker which is sited in the cloakroom area. A 'pinger' is set to indicate when the cakes are ready.

Cooking gives children the opportunity to learn, in a practical way, about balance and the necessity for accuracy in weighing. It indicates the need to read instructions carefully, otherwise the cakes are not very appetizing. It provides sensory experience of various kinds – sight, smell and taste – and gives opportunities for discrimination about texture and consistency. Transferring the mixture from mixing bowl to cake tins helps children to construct their understanding of volume. When the cakes are placed in the oven and the pinger is set the children have a practical experience of the passage of time. When the cakes are ready the sharing of the finished product provides the beginning of understanding of this aspect of division. Supposing there are sixteen small cakes to be shared by a group of five cooks – what does one do about the one left over? Here is the problem of the 'remainder' in a practical situation. How does one solve it? Does one give it to the teacher or divide it into five pieces? How does one find a fifth of a cake? Here are numerous opportunities for questions and answers, for surmise and discussion.

Cooking is a social activity involving group cooperation and the amount of conversation which arises throughout is tremendous. It provides opportunity for vocabulary extension by the introduction of new words, as in the case of two small girls who came across the instruction 'Take an extra egg' in their recipe. Not knowing what 'extra' meant they approached an older boy on his way to the woodwork bench and asked him to explain. 'It means another one, silly' he said, and went on about his business. New meanings of known words become clear as when a cake is referred to as being 'light' — light in texture as opposed to light in weight. What is more, cooking is fun, and the end product enjoyable.

In this classroom, cooking was introduced by the teacher giving a demonstration. The children gathered round and watched while she went through the various stages, beginning with the important preparation of washing her hands and putting on a clean apron. As she mixed she talked and the children asked questions. The small cakes when baked were shared out and everyone had a taste. The teacher then said that if the children wished to cook, a small group could do so each day. Next day some of the children arrived complete with ingredients which they had brought from home. These were augmented by materials bought through school funds. Small groups were allowed to cook each day under strict supervision either by the teacher or the ancillary, but before the year was out the children became so responsible in attitude, and practised in technique, that they did all the preparations themselves and merely asked for adult help in putting the cakes in the oven and removing them when baked. As there were three classes in the unit, it meant that a group from one class baked in the morning, a group from another class baked in the afternoon, and the third class had its turn on the following morning. It was therefore some time before everyone had had their turn at cooking.

Cleaning up is always part of the exercise and the children, after placing their cakes in the oven, return to the classroom, clear away any mess they have made, wash their utensils and put them away, replace their aprons and move on to the next activity.

Two other children meanwhile may be working at the sink (2) on an assignment concerned with capacity, and a group of four or five may be engaged on a model connected with a class project (3): others may be painting or working on a piece of collage. The fixed worktop (4) at this end of the room is usually reserved for displays and the display panel over the heater is linked with this. On one occasion a model of The Magic Roundabout held pride of place here. A small boy had brought a home-made model of Dougal to school and the comments of the other children indicated a common interest in this television series. The teacher and a group of children examined the model to find out how it was made, and decided they could make the other characters from similar materials. Each child chose which character he would make, and the group set to work.

Lively discussion followed as the children sorted through the materials provided for their use, to find the appropriate colours and textures for garments, footwear, hats and hair. From time to time the teacher came to see how things were progressing. Advice and friendly criticism were meted out freely within the group and each child strove to meet the requirements and standards of the others. The results were admirable. Attention was then given to the background: trees, flowers and leaves were produced and painted and arranged on the worktop, and the characters grouped artistically among the trees. The whole was much admired by the rest of the class.

The teacher then suggested that some of the class might like to make their own Dougal story. A small group opted to do this and when they had decided on the plot the teacher wrote captions in bold felt-pen script to the children's dictation. Others proceeded to paint illustrations to fit the captions and when the story was complete, pictures and captions were stuck together to form a continuous roll. With the aid of a large cardboard carton and two lengths of dowelling a make-believe television set was constructed. The two ends of the 'story' were attached to the rods with the majority of the material rolled on to the bottom one. This left the first picture and caption on display. When this had been read, the top rod was turned until the next picture and caption appeared, and so the story unrolled. This became a favourite class 'reader' and children were often observed rolling the picture round and reading their own TV story.

The round table (5) beyond the low cupboard is the place where small groups are gathered together by the teacher for direct teaching. From time to time during the day children are found here engaged on such ploys as phonic games, or a practice with flash cards, or some explanation of a maths process, or discussion about work done, or a new group project. At times when this table is not required for such purposes children may use it for recording, or as an overflow from the art/craft area.

Four or five children may also be working in the maths area (6) dealing with concrete materials, experimenting, solving problems and recording their findings. Assignment cards prepared by the teacher and protected with self-adhesive plastic sheeting are colour-coded according to difficulty in all the areas of measurement, and cover also such topics as shape, size, symmetry, area, ratio etc. These cards are kept in pockets or boxes so that the children can help themselves as required. Care has been given to provide extra practice cards for those children who need more experience in order to consolidate understanding. Equipment of all kinds such as balances, scales, metric measures, tapes, trundle wheels, metric containers, timing devices, and real money is available as well as all sorts of arbitrary measures. A large variety of objects for sorting and classifying with sorting trays (which in this case are seed trays bought from a local garden shop in a sale) are also available, as are sets of logiblocks, poleidoblocks and so on. The teachers in this school have worked out the sort of activities they consider necessary for the children to acquire essential experience and to build up concepts, and there is a clearly defined progression in each aspect of mathematics. In addition, mathematics can also arise incidentally from the children's interests and the themes and projects on which they are working. Records which indicate the stages through which each child has passed are kept, and the teachers believe also in talking with each child or group of children about what they are doing or have done, in order to discover what the processes of thinking have been and how each solution has been reached. In this way the teachers can ascertain where understanding has been achieved, or where children need more practice in order to further understanding. As each child has arrived at school with his own peculiar pre-school experiences, this kind of oral checking by the teacher has to be done at individual level. She cannot assume that any two children will have had identical preparation, and only through observation of the child at work or play, and by talking to him can she assess his present position and know how and when to help him develop his learning.

Some children may be in the home play area (7), partitioned off in this case by the use of one of the free-standing cupboards. Here there is a table and some chairs, a play cooker, a dresser with plastic cutlery and crockery, a washing-up bowl, some dolls, a doll's bed and dressing-up clothes. There is a washing line outside and on fine days the children may be seen washing the doll's clothes and hanging them out to dry — a useful way of suggesting that clothes need to be kept clean. In the home play area children gain incidental experience of a one-to-one relationship when they set the table — one for Daddy, one for Mummy, one for Peter and one for me. The dresser is clearly labelled with the names of various items so that children put the plates on one pile, saucers on another, hang the cups on hooks, and place the egg-cups in their appointed place. Similarly the saucepans and the colander have places allocated to them. In this way the children learn to put things away tidily and begin to sort and classify, and count in the process.

The dressing-up trolley provides the clues for all sorts of different adult roles — the bus driver, the ambulance driver, the fireman, the doctor, the nurse and the policeman as well as mother and father. This area gives endless opportunities for children to assume adult roles and project themselves into imaginary situations. It provides an outlet for social and emotional difficulties and, depending on the provision and intervention of the teacher, presents opportunities for a great variety of experience and language development. Dressing-up clothes in this classroom are kept on hangers and frequently washed and ironed so that they always look attractive and well-kept.

The display tables (8) with pinboard over always have something colourful or interesting on them to attract attention. Sometimes there is a selection of rocks or shells, at others a beautiful drape forms the background for a colour collection, sometimes there is a nature display and sometimes a display aimed at some kind of sensory discrimination. Each display will be purposeful and intended to stimulate interest and talk, and will be changed when the teacher senses that a new stimulus is needed.

In the reading corner (9) a square of carpet gives a homely feel and some large square paint tins have been covered with bright foam-backed material forming attractive child-sized stools. There are story books and picture books, poetry books, books with information, and word books of different types set out on the shelves and racks. Here two or three children may be seen sitting simply looking at books or being read to by a more able reader.

Next to the reading corner is the writing/recording area so that it is easy to look up the spelling of a word one needs to use, or to seek a piece of information required when recording something of interest. Here all sorts and sizes of writing papers, plain and lined, white and coloured, are provided with a selection of pencils, black and coloured, crayons thick and thin, biros and fibre-tipped pens of various shades, all intended to make writing an attractive pastime, and to enable work to be presented as well as possible. Here too are pockets containing cards with writing patterns to copy, questions to answer, pictures to describe or to start off a story, missing word games and simple crossword puzzles. There are word lists and dictionaries and usually a display of writing connected with art work. A visit to the fair may have resulted in models of acrobats flying through hoops, of clowns turning somersaults and horses prancing. These are discussed and may well result in written work. Often here a child will look at another's work and be inspired to try something himself either in the same medium or perhaps in quite another.

In the centre of the room a group of children may be building a castle from large construction blocks, or making a helicopter from old cartons and boxes, or stuffing a figure made from an old sack and some nylon stockings, or experimenting with tuned percussion or there may be a group with the teacher working on the floor with hoops and logiblocks. The activities are constantly changing as the need arises.

Just inside the door is a table with four chairs: this is where the children drink their milk. The table is set with mats, the crate of bottles is near at hand and the children are at liberty to drink their milk as and when they wish during the morning – that is as long as there is a chair vacant. This is intended to be a social occasion and the children are expected to behave in a civilized manner.

Outside in the cloakroom area, which is quite spacious, a group of children may be working at the woodwork bench, or at the experimental music trolley alongside the old piano. This old piano, which was donated by a parent, is intended for the children's use. They can remove the front to see how it works and try out tunes (with one or more fingers) with impunity. They know that the new piano in the hall is for adult use only. These activities set up in the cloakroom are shared by all three classes. There is also a piece of bare wall above the coat racks where each class in turn produces a wall story. The pictures are painted by the children and the captions written by the teacher – a useful cooperative reading situation. Doors to the classrooms are usually open but if the noise of hammering or experimental music becomes too obtrusive, either the doors are closed or the noisy activities cease for a time by mutual consent.

The teachers in these three classrooms work well together. Each uses her own version of an 'integrated day' although the three classrooms are all arranged differently. Each has a particular skill, one being gifted artistically, one being specially interested in mathematics and the other in language development, and they help and advise one another. Children can move from one classroom to another to join in certain activities. For instance, different art activities are set up in the three rooms and if a child wants to use clay and it is not provided in his own room on that day, he can find it in another room. At times the three classes may decide to have a singing session together. One teacher plays the piano, another will direct operations, and the third may well withdraw a group of her own children to whom she wishes to give extra time and attention. Sometimes the three teachers decide on a theme on which all three classes can work and together produce a display to which the rest of the school can be invited. In this school, teachers walk in and out of each other's rooms and comment on what they see, and this too results in a pooling of ideas. In one such case a teacher from another room commented on a display of 3D shapes which the children had arranged on a display panel. She remarked that it looked like a fantastic machine. The children overheard her comment and proceeded to turn the display into a machine by adding string and rubber bands from shape to shape, so making them move. This inspired other children to make a whole range of machines from junk, and to paint pictures of machines and to write descriptions about how they worked. Nearly everyone in the class contributed something and finally a group of girls wrote a poem about machines, and then made it into a song which they accompanied on tuned percussion (Plummer 1969).

The casual visitor might imagine that the children in this room are completely free to do as they like. In fact for a classroom to run on these lines successfully, a great deal of planning, organization and preparation is required on the part of the teacher. Children are free within limits and these limits are imposed in the first place by the provision that is made. Then there are two rules which must be kept: these are that one considers other people, and that one respects apparatus and equipment. The children know that certain standards are expected of them in terms of behaviour and they respond to these expectations. They learn that they can only be 'free' in relation to other people's freedom and that this requires self-discipline. They learn through experience to accept frustration, to give and take, and to take their turn. There is a feeling of mutual respect between teachers and pupils, and the children learn a great deal from the teachers' example.

A certain amount of distrust of so-called 'modern methods' has developed in some areas, resulting in criticism in the press and elsewhere. At one time people were given the impression that it was enough for teachers to provide an interesting and stimulating environment in which children would develop naturally and spontaneously. It was thought that the child's own interests would lead him to experiment with the materials and apparatus provided, to enquire and explore, to make discoveries, and to solve problems. The message to the teacher seemed to be 'Let the child develop naturally'. Some teachers who tried this approach (perhaps having been misled about what their role should be), and who, having created the stimulating environment, left the children very much to their own devices,

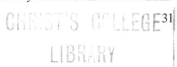

not surprisingly became dissatisfied with results and rejected 'modern methods' as unsatisfactory. Observers of such practice and its results also tend to blame the methods. It is, of course, in the misunderstanding and not in the methods that the fault lies.

A large number of children, if left entirely to their own devices in a stimulating environment, may learn very little. Teachers have come to realize that for many children (depending on their previous experience and all-round development) some degree of guidance and help from the teacher is necessary if activities are to prove productive and purposeful. This realization has resulted in classroom organization and techniques such as are described here. The flexibility that is apparent in classrooms such as this has developed from a highly structured situation where the teacher knows her children, their needs and their capabilities, and makes appropriate provision for them. Such a way of working is not achieved overnight and often evolves through the stages mentioned in Chapter 1.

References

PLUMMER, C. M. (1969) A reader's contribution *Child Education* Vol. 46, No. 1

3 Moving into the new school

Figure 12 (page 34) shows a replacement school built to accommodate 280 junior mixed and infant children. It is a church aided school and has some community provision. The church is reached by a covered way. The community has the use of the hall, kitchen and enclosable room, termed quiet/noisy room on the plan. Access to the rest of the school building in the evenings is cut off by lockable double doors.

The main entrance lies between the hall and the administrative block, and the passage which is well over six feet wide provides waiting space for visitors. Off this passage there is a small office for the school secretary. The headteacher's room lies beyond and is separated from the staffroom by a folding screen wall which enables both rooms to be opened up for staff meetings, managers' meetings and the like. The central store opens off the staffroom, and a caretaker's store and staff lavatories are also provided in this block.

The teaching area has been planned in three units round a central courtyard – the fourth side being occupied by the hall and enclosable room. There are eight home bases and the three units have been designed to hold 105, 70 and 105 children respectively. Thus two units have three home bases and the third has two. In the two larger units the home bases have, in this case, been designed to allow greater flexibility in use than is possible in some other plans. Some teachers do not like a cooperative teaching situation and here bases 3 and 6 have been designed to open away from the general activity area, so that the teachers occupying those particular spaces can, if they wish, work entirely on their own, or join in for part of the day only. The design does not, however, prevent complete cooperation if the teachers so desire. Access to the outside is possible either through double doors in Units 1 and 3 or through the cloaks areas.

Bases 4 and 5 are separated in this plan by a movable screen wall which again allows flexibility in use. The two bases can be used entirely separately or, if a larger group space is required, the central wall can be rolled back. If the doors to the bays are then closed, a sizeable room suitable for class activities is formed. This room can also be used by Units 1 and 3 when available.

The library/resource area is located centrally in Unit 2 and children

Figure 12

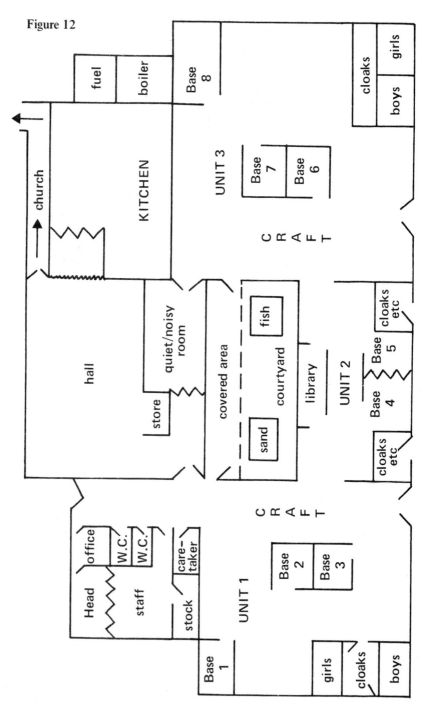

from Units 1 and 3 have easy access to it. Similarly the craft facilities in Units 1 and 3 are accessible to the children in Unit 2. This plan provides for children from the various units to mix if the need arises.

A quiet/noisy room for activities such as singing, instrumental work, drama, television and radio programmes, slide/tape programmes, French lessons, class lessons and for silent study has been provided. This is cut off from the units by lockable doors, and from the hall entrance by a movable wooden partition. This room can be used by the community as a committee room in the evenings.

There is access to the central courtyard from Units 1 and 3. Part of this courtyard is covered and houses work-benches and shelters the school pets. There is also a covered sand-pit and a fish-pool. Trees and flowering shrubs give shade and colour, and seats have been provided. Noisy craft activities are thus situated away from the main work area yet are still under supervision and pets are safe from vandalism.

The kitchen is separated from the hall by sliding doors. Meals are served in the hall in two sittings and the quiet/noisy room can also be used for meals if required. A store for physical education apparatus and equipment is provided off the hall and meals furniture is stored beyond the sliding doors.

Allocation of space

The school has been designed to accommodate 280 children aged five to eleven years in eight class groups with a pupil/teacher ratio of 35:1. As easy access from unit to unit is desirable for the children, possibly the best distribution would be to place three classes of infants in Unit 1, the younger juniors in Unit 2 and the oldest juniors in Unit 3. This arrangement would enable children in Units 1 and 2 to move from one area to the other as needed. For example, lower juniors who find difficulty with reading could move into Unit 1 for certain language experiences and the more able members of Unit 1 who require the stimulus of older children could work from time to time in Unit 2. Similarly children in Units 2 and 3 could interchange or cooperate as required. This system of organization also demonstrates a logical progression through the building as the child grows older. It also places the oldest children, who will probably need it most often, nearest to the enclosable room.

Allocation of children

The school is due for occupation in September next. At the time of transfer there will be the following numbers of children:

157 juniors: 39 children aged 10+
                 42 children aged 9+
                 40 children aged 8+
                 36 children aged 7+

102 infants: 41 children aged 6+
              40 children aged 5+
              21 children of 5 years of age to be admitted in September

              9 children of 5 years of age to be admitted in January;
              12 children of 5 years of age to be admitted in April

Total   280 children

Obviously year groups do not fit tidily into the ratio 35:1 and a solution to the problem must be found. The most practical solution perhaps is to start with the oldest children and work downwards. The following pattern of organization then emerges:

class A   35 oldest 4th year juniors
class B   4 youngest 4th year juniors + 31 oldest 3rd year juniors
class C   11 youngest 3rd year juniors + 24 oldest 2nd year juniors
class D   16 youngest 2nd year juniors + 19 oldest 1st year juniors
class E   17 youngest 1st year juniors + 18 oldest infants
Total   83 + 92 = 175 children

This completes the organization of Units 3 and 2 and has the advantage of keeping the children in each class within a year's age span.
    In September there will be:

              23 youngest six year old infants
              40 five year olds
              21 new admissions
Total   84 children

    There appear to be three alternative ways of organizing Unit 1 (infants):

1 To continue the downward pattern as follows:
    class F   23 youngest six year old infants + 12 oldest five year olds
    class G   28 youngest five year old infants + 6 admissions
    class H   15 remaining admissions + 9 entrants in January
                   + 12 entrants in April
    Total   66 + 39 = 105 children

2 A form of transitional vertical grouping:
    class F   23 youngest six year olds + 12 oldest five year olds as
              before
    class G   14 of the oldest five year olds + 11 September admissions
              + 4 January admissions + 6 April admissions
    class H   14 of the oldest five year olds + 10 September admissions
              + 5 January admissions + 6 April admissions
    Total   51 + 33 + 9 + 12 = 105 children

3 Vertical grouping throughout the Unit:

class F   8 of the youngest six year olds + 13 five year olds
            + 7 September entrants + 3 January entrants
            + 4 April entrants

class G   8 of the youngest six year olds + 13 five year olds
            + 7 September entrants + 3 January entrants
            + 4 April entrants

class H   7 of the youngest six year olds + 14 five year olds
            + 7 September entrants + 3 January entrants
            4 April entrants

Total   23 + 40 + 21 + 9 + 12 = 105 children

There are, of course, a number of alternative ways of organizing the school, some of which are shown below:

1 Full vertical grouping throughout Units 2 and 3 as follows:

class A   8 (aged 10+) + 8 (aged 9+) + 8 (aged 8+) + 8 (aged 7+)
            + 3 (oldest infants) = 35

class B   8 (aged 10+) + 8 (aged 9+) + 8 (aged 8+) + 7 (aged 7+)
            + 4 (oldest infants) = 35

class C   8 (aged 10+) + 8 (aged 9+) + 8 (aged 8+) + 7 (aged 7+)
            + 4 (oldest infants) = 35

class D   8 (aged 10+) + 9 (aged 9+) + 8 (aged 8+) + 7 (aged 7+)
            + 3 (oldest infants) = 35

class E   7 (aged 10+) + 9 (aged 9+) + 8 (aged 8+) + 7 (aged 7+)
            + 4 (oldest infants) = 35

Total   39 + 42 + 40 + 36 + 18 = 175 children

2 With Unit 1 organized in one of the ways described above (1, 2 or 3) and vertical grouping within the units as follows:

Unit 3   class A   13 (aged 10+) + 14 (aged 9+) + 8 (oldest eight year olds) = 35
           class B   13 (aged 10+) + 14 (aged 9+) + 8 (oldest eight year olds) = 35
           class C   13 (aged 10+) + 14 (aged 9+) + 8 (oldest eight year olds) = 35

Total   39 + 42 + 24 = 105 children

Unit 2   class D   8 (youngest 8+) + 18 (aged 7+) + 9 (oldest 6+) = 35
           class E   8 (youngest 8+) + 18 (aged 7+) + 9 (oldest 6+) = 35

Total   16 + 36 + 18 = 70 children

3 Vertical grouping over 2 years and class A as an age group as follows:

class A   35 (oldest ten years olds)

class B   2 (youngest 10+) + 21 (aged 9+) + 12 (oldest eight year olds) = 35

class C   2 (youngest 10+) + 21 (aged 9+) + 12 (oldest
            eight year olds) = 35
Total   105 children
classes D and E vertically grouped as in 2 and Unit 1 organized in one
of the ways described originally.

4 Units 1 and 3 organized as originally suggested, and Unit 2 as in 2.

5 To keep to the four year groups as much as possible in the junior
   Units 2 and 3, removing the less able from each year group so that
   classes of 35 remain. The less able children each year would then be
   formed into a remedial class occupying base 4. The result would be:
   class A   35 ten year olds
   class B   35 nine year olds
   class C   35 eight year olds
   class D   35 seven year olds
   remedial class E   4 (less able 10+) + 7 (least able 9+) + 5 (least
                      able 8+) + 1 (least able 7+) = 17

   This would result in all the infant children being accommodated in
   Unit 1. This Unit built for 105 children would then house 102 children
   in the Autumn term, 111 in the Spring term and 123 in the Summer
   term, resulting in three class groups of 34 children in the first term, 37
   in the second term and 41 in the third term, and is not a desirable
   solution.

6 Another solution might be to commence the year as suggested in 5, and
   in order to overcome the undesirable overcrowding and large classes in
   the infant department, to 'promote' the oldest children in each group
   to the next group each term to make room for the entrants, while still
   retaining the remedial group. This could simply result in removing the
   problem of overcrowding from the infant department to the junior
   department and has the added disadvantage of disrupting every class in
   the school each term.

7 Still another solution some people might favour would be to commence
   the school year with the 259 children then on roll divided into eight
   more or less equal groups with the youngest in a reception class as
   follows:

   in September class A   33 (4th year juniors)
                 class B   6 (4th year juniors) + 27 (3rd year juniors)
                 class C   15 (3rd year juniors) + 17 (2nd year juniors)
                 class D   23 (2nd year juniors) + 9 (1st year juniors)
                 class E   27 (1st year juniors) + 6 (children of 6+)
                 class F   33 (children of 6+)

class G   2 (children of 6+) + 31 (children of 5+)
class H   9 (children of 5+) + 21 (entrants aged 5)
Total   148 + 111 = 259 children

In January when 9 entrants are admitted to Class H the 9 oldest children move into Class G. To accommodate them 9 are moved from Class G into Class F and so on throughout the school. The process is repeated in April to accommodate the 12 children due for admission then. Again each class is disrupted each term – a practice which is not desirable.

There are other permutations. The problem is which solution to choose.

What are the needs of the children?

1   Security and stability are high on the list of priorities. Primary school children need to be able to make stable relationships with their teachers, and the teachers need time in which to get to know the children, to understand them and to assess their requirements, in order to deal adequately with them. Each child is unique, and has needs peculiar to him. Therefore, to be really successful and productive the relationship between teacher and child needs to be as long as possible. The observant and perceptive teacher will then be able to meet the needs of each individual within the group. The younger the child, the more he needs this close relationship with one particular person, while still being able to meet other adults within the school. It seems, therefore, beneficial for both teacher and children to be together for at least a year. Hence any system of organization which entails promotion within a year, and particularly in the first year of schooling, is to be avoided if possible.

2   Most primary children, we are told, are not yet at the stage of abstract thinking. They need concrete materials with which to work, and the younger the child the more he needs access to concrete materials. Because infants are usually smaller physically than juniors, it is sometimes thought that they take up less room and, therefore, need less room. In fact the younger the child the more room he needs in which to operate. The infant's span of concentration is shorter and there is a greater need for a variety of activities to be always available to keep him interested and purposefully occupied. Any form of organization which deprives the young child of room in which to move should be avoided if possible.

3   Primary school children need opportunities to develop their powers of thinking through experience, enquiry and experiment. They need to have recourse to all sorts of sources of reference including the teacher. Older children who are able to read and write can find out a good deal for themselves under the guidance of the teacher, and the teacher can assess, up to a point, the extent of the child's understanding, from his

written work. The younger the child, however, the more he needs access to the teacher. She is his main source of reference, until he can read, and she must be available when required. In her turn the teacher can most easily assess the young child's understanding by talking to him and observing what he does. A form of organization which keeps numbers in class as small as possible in the early years of schooling is to be encouraged.

4   Entrants have special needs. The change from home to school can be a traumatic experience, and every effort should be made to make this transfer as easy as possible. A reception class is perhaps not the best situation for these small children. None of the children are *au fait* with the situation – the room is strange, the teacher is strange and the other children are strange. He has forgotten, in his distress, where the lavatory is situated, where his outdoor clothes are to be found, and he wants to go home. He is emotionally upset, and cannot give his mind to any of the interesting things around him for this reason. Each entrant needs to feel that he can call on the full attention of the adults to whom he is entrusted in this strange place, and where there is a reception class of twenty or thirty small children all in the same stage of initiation, this is well-nigh impossible. The teacher is hard pressed if she attempts to meet the needs of twenty such individuals. One crying infant will soon infect others in the group and the first week or two in school can be a trying and unpleasant experience for teacher and children alike. When entrants can be distributed amongst two or three classes, in which there are already children who are well acquainted with the environment, each teacher is able to give more individual attention where and when it is required. A form of organization which allows this is to be encouraged.

How entrants may be helped

The special needs of entrants are more widely recognized nowadays. More and more schools are making pre-school visits available in the term before children are due for admission. These vary both in nature and number.

Some headteachers invite mothers to bring their children to the school on one afternoon in the last two or three weeks of the term. In some cases children sit with their parents while the headteacher explains some of the things mothers can do to prepare their children for school – a boring process for the children and information which is probably too late to be of much use to the mother.

Other headteachers invite small groups of children to come with their parents on several days so that visits are staggered. Parents and children then go to the classrooms to which the children are to be allocated when admitted. Where vertical grouping is used this means that the child meets his teacher, and his future classmates, and becomes familiar with his new

40

classroom. Sometimes the visit is for the whole afternoon and the mother is encouraged to stay with the child in the classroom until break. After break the child stays in the classroom while the parents join the headteacher for a question and answer session.

In some schools this pattern is repeated throughout the term and some morning visits are also arranged. The staggering of visits means that only small groups of visitors are involved at any one time, so that this does not impose too heavy a burden on any class or teacher. Parents are encouraged to stay and play with their children until they appear to have settled. This has the advantage of allowing the child to settle in a situation shared with his mother, and gives the mother an opportunity to become acquainted with what goes on in a modern infant classroom.

In some cases headteachers invite parents to bring their children regularly every week to a 'pre-reception' group. The headteacher and welfare ancillary set up activities in the hall on one afternoon each week, and parents and children are invited to take part. The children become used to the school and its facilities and learn how to use certain materials and apparatus, to play with bricks, blocks and home-play equipment, all with a sense of security engendered by having their mothers with them. There are nursery rhymes to say and sing, and stories to hear. Towards the end of the term mothers are asked to stay on a rota system, so that gradually the children become used to staying in school without mother being there. Finally in the last two weeks of term the children join the classes to which they will be allocated as entrants.

When the new term begins the children arrive already familiar with the classroom, the teacher and the other children, and with the layout and routine of the school, making the final transfer from home to school as painless as possible. In spite of this preparation, however, full-time attendance can still be quite an ordeal and the children still need as much individual attention as possible. Many schools arrange staggered admission by appointment. This means that each entrant is welcomed separately into the class and is ensured of the teacher's whole attention for a period. Again, practice varies. Some schools stagger admissions over a morning, some over a day, some over a week or ten days, while a few schools believe it is so important that each entrant should be welcomed properly that entrance on the fifth birthday or on the first school day following the fifth birthday is stipulated. Admission in this case is staggered throughout the year.

Even with the expansion of nursery provision in the offing, there will be a number of children whose parents prefer not to send them to school permanently before the age of five. These children will still need preparation for entry. Where nursery provision is separate from the primary school, ways of assisting transfer from one situation to the other will need to be found. It will still be necessary, therefore, for schools to make admission as pleasant as possible, so that entrants settle in easily and are able to take advantage of the learning situation as quickly as possible.

Vertical grouping

Some form of vertical grouping is undoubtedly beneficial at infant level, both from the point of view of the teacher and of the children. Entrants settle more quickly and easily into a situation where not only the teacher, but other children know the geography of the classroom and the school, and can show the newcomers where to find things or where to go at various times during the day. Often an older child has an entrant allocated to him/her for the first week or two, and welcomes the responsibility of looking after the newcomer. He has to see that the child visits the lavatory at break times, and help him on with outdoor clothes, or help him change for physical education, and see that he is in the right place at the right time. A fortnight is usually long enough for this exercise. By this time most entrants have become self-sufficient and two weeks is long enough for the older child to be involved in this way. Otherwise what was welcomed as a sign of the teacher's approval becomes a bore and a source of frustration. The help of older children in this way enables the teacher to give her attention and help in other directions.

Routines and attitudes then, are learnt as much from older children in the class as from the teacher. Because group and individual methods are used of necessity in a vertically grouped situation it is also possible for the young child to learn almost incidentally from the activities of older or more able children. For instance two or three entrants might be engaged in building with blocks near to a group of older children who are playing a phonic game with the teacher. Part of their attention may well be given to the older children's activity and when their turn comes to be introduced to phonics they recognize the sound more readily. Or if a younger child demonstrates his ability to assimilate what the older children are learning he can be encouraged to join them for that activity, rejoining his own group for other forms of learning.

There is a further advantage in the fact that children remain with the same teacher for a longer period, thus precluding the necessity for making new relationships with a new teacher in a new situation too often. It takes quite a time for some children to make a good relationship with the teacher and other children in the class, and until he is socially and emotionally secure he does not begin to learn. This is why promotion during the school year is considered unwise. Where this happens, a child who may have been admitted to a reception class will have taken until half-term to settle in and be making some progress in the second half of the term, only to be moved on to the next class where he has to begin the whole process again. This results in the child making little or no progress in the new class for four or five weeks again, and in some cases there is actual regression. Where this transfer from class to class happens again and again, the process can result in quite serious retardation.

Vertical grouping also allows the teacher to get to know the parents over a longer period of time, and to make better relationships with them. The child who is torn between pleasing his parents and pleasing his teacher is not in an enviable position. If, however, parents and teacher can talk to each other and share their concern for the well-being of the child, then the child is bound to benefit.

Parents are rightly concerned that their children receive the best education possible. Their judgment of what is 'good' educationally is usually based on their own experience. Hence their suspicion of so called 'modern' methods and approaches. Their suspicions are usually allayed when they receive assurance that the teacher too is concerned that each child receives the education best suited to his needs, and that methods and approaches used are educationally sound. When the term vertical grouping is introduced at a parents' meeting someone invariably raises the question of what happens to the child who is placed with a 'weak' teacher for the whole of his infant career.

This is a valid criticism of the system and highlights the only real disadvantage of vertical grouping. However, the headteacher who recognizes that certain members of staff have certain weaknesses, can compensate by placing the child with a teacher who has comparable strengths for the next part of his school career. Alternatively the headteacher might be well advised to shorten the period of time which children spend with any one teacher, and employ a form of transitional vertical grouping rather than full vertical grouping. (See *Allocation of children; unit 1, (infants) alternative 2 page 36.*) A third solution to this problem which is possible in a vertically grouped situation, and which is particularly appropriate where a child and a teacher appear to be incompatible is to transfer the child to a parallel class.

There are teachers as well as parents who view this system with some concern and are convinced, even though they already use a flexible approach geared to the needs of each individual, that the wider age range presents insuperable difficulties. Full vertical grouping is probably not appropriate where staff hold such strong misgivings, and transitional vertical grouping would, in such a case, be preferable. Having attempted transitional vertical grouping with no ill-effects these teachers might then be prepared to move on to a system of full vertical grouping with equal success. Teachers as well as children need to feel secure.

More infant teachers than junior teachers have had experience of some form of vertical grouping. It needs an expert and experienced teacher to deal really successfully with a class of thirty-five children whose ages range from seven to eleven years. This age range occurs naturally in some small village schools but class numbers in those cases are usually smaller. When introducing vertical grouping to the junior department it is probably wiser to keep to a maximum age range of two years initially.

Allocation of children to vertical groups

There are two main ways of allocating children to vertical groups — either random selection or selection by ability.

One knows comparatively little about entrants with any certainty other than age and sex, and this lack of knowledge precludes any attempt to group them according to ability. Most infant headteachers then use some form of random selection while trying to keep a balance in each group as far as age and sex are concerned. It follows quite by chance that occasionally some groups are more able than others, although usually a comparable spread of ability is achieved in each group. If there appears to be a concentration of more able or less able children in any one group, however, transitional vertical grouping provides some redress. When the older children are regrouped for their final year in the infant school/ department, they can be allocated to their new classes according to the ability shown in their first class groups, enabling true mixed-ability classes to be formed.

Vertical grouping in the junior department can use either form of selection. The headteacher has the option of grouping according to the ability shown in the infant stage, or deliberately choosing to use random selection.

It should be pointed out that vertical grouping and vertical streaming are not identical. Vertical streaming groups children of a two year age range, on comparable ability so that the more able children from both years are allocated to one group and the less able from both years to another group. However, research has indicated that mixed-ability groups are beneficial socially and emotionally and can be beneficial intellectually also. An American study (Goldberg *et al* 1961) indicates that children in mixed-ability groups tend to work towards the middle range of ability. If this is true then 50 per cent of the children must benefit intellectually from this kind of grouping. It would appear that the more able 50 per cent might be adversely affected from such grouping. However, an experienced teacher who is aware of this tendency, and who gears the children's work to the needs of each individual, would presumably make sure that the more able children were encouraged to work to the top limits of their ability. This in turn should benefit the rest of the children. In the past perhaps teachers have tended to be concerned about the less able members of the class to the detriment of the very able. This research emphasizes the necessity of giving every child his fair share of attention at his own level of ability.

Allocation of staff

There is a staff of headteacher, eight full-time teachers, and a .5 part-time teacher. The new school establishment provides for a deputy head, one Scale 3 post and two Scale 2 posts. There is to be one full-time welfare ancillary and a part-time clerk.

The headteacher in this case is a woman aged forty. She is married with one child. She is junior trained and four years ago was seconded for a year's Diploma in Education course at the local university, and has been at this school for the past three years. She is particularly interested in learning theories.

The present deputy head, a man in charge of fourth year juniors, is retiring at Easter. Another member of staff, a young married woman, is leaving to have a baby. She has elected to go at the end of the Spring term also. She held a scale post and taught in the infant department. The remainder of the staff are as follows:

Mr Smith, aged 35. Married with three children. Is in his second year of teaching, having previously been a policeman. He is a quiet, gentle type (who can, however, be obstinate at times), and is usually receptive to advice and help from the head. He did well in his college course and specialized in language development. He is junior trained but anxious to get on in his new profession and is interested in the development of first schools. He is keen to gain experience of teaching young children and has asked to be transferred to the infant department.

Mrs Jones, aged 33. Married with two children. She is a pleasant person with a bright cheerful manner (who can on the odd occasion demonstrate a quick temper). She is liked and respected by her colleagues, the children and the parents. She is scrupulously fair in her dealings with children – a quality they like; is interested in creative activities and has a flair in this direction. Her enthusiasm is infectious. She has been at the school for five years; is infant/junior trained. She has a Scale 2 post but is not ambitious.

Miss Brown, aged 43. Has a widowed invalid mother to support and has no outside interests as the school and her home take all her time and energy. She is hardworking and dependable but has little imagination and is traditional in outlook and method. She is extremely apprehensive about the open plan situation. She has been at this school for eleven years and for six years has been responsible for girls' needlework. She is expecting to receive a scale post for her interest in needlework and her long service. She is junior trained.

Mrs Wright, aged 31. Married with no children. She has moved to this area because of her husband's promotion, and has been in the school for one term. She held a Scale 2 post in her previous school. She has a diploma in Primary Education, having specialized in child development. Is clearly above average in ability. She is progressive in outlook and cares a great deal for children. A good all-rounder. She also speaks fluent French and is infant/junior trained.

Mr Robinson, aged 26. Single. Was appointed a year ago having transferred from secondary school where he was a member of the craft department. He is junior/secondary trained. Clearly disenchanted with the secondary scene, he has not as yet fully adjusted to primary work and has shown no wish to develop his craft interest at junior level. He is beginning to show some aptitude for physical education and is prepared to stay after school hours for sporting activities. So far he has shown little interest in attending courses at the local teachers' centre.

Mrs Taylor, aged 45. Married with one teenaged daughter. Is junior trained. A pleasant placid type who gets on well with everyone. Five years ago she was seconded for a term's course on primary maths. She is also musical, is hardworking and loyal, and has been at the school for seven years. She holds a Scale 2 post.

Mrs Johnson, aged 46. A .5 part-time teacher. Married with two adolescent daughters. Well-meaning and amenable. Junior trained but has no special abilities.

The headteacher has decided that she will have the type of organization described on page 36, i.e. starting with the oldest children and working downwards in the junior units and using the form of transitional vertical grouping suggested for the infant unit.

From her knowledge of the qualities and attributes of the staff, the headteacher has decided to place Mrs Jones (Scale 2) and Mrs Wright in charge of the two vertical groups in the infant unit, Mrs Wright has also offered to teach some French to the oldest juniors after 3.30 pm. After due consideration the head has agreed to Mr Smith's request for a transfer to the infant department. She feels that his understanding of children will allow him to adjust to the needs of small children. She is also of the opinion that the infants will probably benefit from having a man with whom to relate. Mr Smith will be in charge of class F with the opportunity to work separately or cooperatively in the unit as required.

The head has decided to place Miss Brown with class A – the oldest juniors – where her traditional methods and approach will affect the school least, and where her insistence on hard work and good standards will be appreciated. Mrs Taylor is to be placed with class C in Unit 1 and Mr Robinson in class D in Unit 2.

The head has decided to advertise for a woman deputy head – a woman with good infant experience, with enthusiasm, qualities of leadership and progressive ideas. This lady will be placed with class E in Unit 2 with the oldest infants and youngest juniors. Here she will be centrally placed and can keep an eye on the infant department and also give help and advice to Mr Robinson. He will now be situated between two teachers of ability and should benefit from their example. Mrs Wright has expressed her intention to apply for this post and Mrs Jones is encouraging her to do so. If no better applicants appear the headteacher feels that Mrs Wright could be a good appointment. She has already shown her ability in the classroom, and has demonstrated intelligence and powers of persuasion in her contributions to staff meetings. If Mrs Wright is appointed deputy head there will then be a vacany in the infant unit. In this case the headteacher has decided to advertise the vacancy in Unit 3 with a Scale 3 post. She will be looking for a teacher with interest and experience in teaching English and creative activities at junior level, or someone who can offer environmental studies as a special interest. She would prefer a man in this position to give some balance. Applications would also be invited from infant teachers used to working in a flexible way for the infant vacancy.

The headteacher has decided against setting up a remedial class. She accepts the fact that many children need extra attention and compensatory education but she also feels that children of above-average ability need their fair share of individual attention and help. She believes that because of his/her understanding of the needs of the children the class teacher is the person best able to give the extra help and attention where it is due. The part-time teacher then is to help out in Units 2 and 3 by taking over certain activities, and releasing the class teacher in turn to give extra time to those children who need it.

The welfare ancillary is to work almost entirely with the infant children. Provision of one full-time welfare ancillary is unrealistic. Ideally each infant class should have its own full-time ancillary. There should at least be a minimum provision of one full-time ancillary for each unit. The headteacher might then decide to use two of these ancillaries to help with infants, allocating the third to the junior department. This would be reasonable as the younger children who rely on spoken language for acquiring information, for reference and communication, need a more favourable child/adult ratio than older children.

Other heads faced with the same situation, might have organized the school and deployed their staff in other ways.

Preparation for the move
The headteacher has had a copy of the final plans and the layout of furniture for some time. Already she and her staff have studied the plan and discussed its possibilities. Her decisions about allocation of space, children and staff have been made in relation to these discussions. At a recent meeting in November she put her decisions to the staff who have agreed and approved them.

The headteacher's approach is a democratic one and she always consults her staff, although, of course, the final decisions and responsibility are hers. She knew, for example, that Miss Brown was hoping for a scale post but wanted to use the Scale 3 post to attract a good candidate for the junior vacancy. Before the staff meeting, therefore, she had a private talk with Miss Brown explaining the position to her fully. The head explained that a Scale 3 post would entail extra duties and that she felt this would be out of the question for Miss Brown with her present commitments. Miss Brown, whilst obviously disappointed, accepted the position, and appreciated the head's tact in approaching her privately. Having procured Miss Brown's agreement the head then felt able to put her decisions to the staff as a whole.

The headteacher has recently received notification of the amount of initial capitation allowance available for the new school. She has asked all the teachers to take stock of their existing apparatus and equipment and to pinpoint areas of need. All recent catalogues have been made available for the staff to make bids for the new equipment they require. Meanwhile the head too is making lists of things she considers necessary. Requisitions will need to be made out well in advance to make sure that new equipment is ready for the move. As the initial allowance is quite generous the head sees the opportunity to purchase some of those items which she cannot normally afford, such as some of the more expensive items of maths equipment, tuned percussion instruments, expensive reference books, one or two cassette tape-recorders, some drapes and ornaments for display, in addition to a greater variety of the necessities like paints, pens and papers.

She has also asked Mrs Taylor, Mrs Wright and Mr Robinson to begin to think out a maths syllabus for use in the new school, commencing with the youngest children where formation of concepts begins and progressing through the school to the oldest and most capable juniors. Mrs Taylor and Mrs Wright are both knowledgeable and capable and Mr Robinson should benefit a great deal from working with them on this project. Not only has she asked them to work out a syllabus but their brief includes making specimen work cards for each stage in the progression in the different aspects of mathematics, and having identified the stages, to produce record cards which can be used for each child throughout his school career.

Similarly, Mrs Jones, Mr Smith and Miss Brown have been asked to suggest themes which can be used for creative activities in different parts of the school, to indicate how these can be developed, and to list the resources necessary to develop them. The headteacher will then visit local bookshops, libraries, and book exhibitions looking for suitable books for the new school library, and will also contact the School Museum Service for information about suitable exhibits. The head also intends working out a graded reading scheme for the school, using existing books and colour-coding them to indicate comparable levels of difficulty. By utilizing all the schemes already available in the school she feels that children will find a wealth of similar material which will allow them plenty of practice. If these are either kept centrally in the library or in each unit, children will be able to go and help themselves to a book at a similar level to one just completed, simply by looking at the colour on the spine.

The head has already asked the staff to begin to think about working together in units. She thinks that probably the best preparation for work in an open plan school is to experiment with more flexible ways of working. Mrs Jones and Mrs Wright are progressive in outlook and already work on 'integrated day' lines. Mr Smith has been more traditional in his approach and has a lot to learn from his infant colleagues. He is prepared to do so and the three have begun to discuss how they can work together in Unit 1. Mrs Wright and Mrs Jones already occupy adjoining rooms separated by a folding partition wall. They have asked the head's permission to open the screens and to work as a unit, commencing in the

Spring term. They have worked out a plan in which each uses the far end of her own room as a home base and for more academic pursuits, and have common use of the central area which is to be used for creative and practical work.

Mrs Jones and Mrs Wright have discussed what they want to do in some detail but have decided to go slowly at first. They realize that they do not teach or run their classes in identical ways and that although their own children are conversant with their own particular system, the children of the other class are not. They have decided, therefore, to spend the first fortnight of the Spring term in a rather formal introduction of the children of both classes to the common creative area. They have agreed to set up four different experiences as follows: (i) painting (ii) clay (iii) collage (iv) paper sculpture. Twelve children from each class will be allowed to use these facilities while the remainder of each class gets on with academic exercises. The children concerned are then shown where to find the various tools and materials they need to use and are also told how to care for their tools and clear up afterwards. Both teachers have agreed on a common standard for preparation and clearing up. When these twenty-four children have been initiated two other sets will take their place, and when all the children have learnt those particular routines other creative activities will be substituted. In this way the teachers hope to prevent muddle and frayed tempers. The headteacher has approved the experiment and has promised that for the period of initiation the welfare ancillary will be at the disposal of these two classes. Meanwhile, Mr Smith is to embark on his own experiment with his present class by introducing the beginnings of a flexible way of working. He has learnt much from the discussions with his future colleagues and accepts that forward planning is essential and he too proposes introducing activities one at a time.

The head has asked Unit 1 to include Mr Robinson in their discussions. He has been very interested in the preliminaries and is beginning to feel more at home with primary work. This, together with his involvement in the maths team, has at least encouraged him to introduce group work in mathematics with his present second-year juniors. He has introduced his class to the concept of ratio first by a class lesson and then setting the children to work on a practical exercise. The results have shown that the children are at very different levels of understanding so he has grouped them roughly according to ability. He is now aiming his work at three broad levels of development and has three largish groups working at different exercises. He intends dividing these groups again, as and when necessary, and expects to have six or seven groups eventually. He realizes that he will need to give those children who need it opportunity for further practice whilst others can be led on to the next step, and that the groups must remain fluid.

Mrs Taylor has used a group topic approach within a subject area for some time. The head has persuaded her that if she can operate groups within a subject area she ought to be able to deal with groups engaged on a variety of subjects. Mrs Taylor is preparing to embark on this approach in the Spring term. She is an experienced teacher, well aware of the pitfalls caused by lack of preparation, and she means to be well-organized before embarking on a new system.

Of the staff due to transfer to the new school, only Miss Brown seems to be doing nothing to prepare herself. Although Miss Brown would never admit her trepidation, the headteacher is fully aware of the extent of her apprehension and is prepared to help her. Miss Brown has the third year juniors at present and will have the advantage of knowing her class extremely well in the new school. This will relieve her of one unknown element. She has been placed where she can, if she wishes, work completely separately, and she has the added advantage of being next door to the enclosable room to which she can withdraw when it is not in use. Miss Brown still uses class teaching methods quite extensively and is afraid to try anything more flexible. She is aware that some children need extra attention and tries to give this when the class is engaged on written work. This means that she has a quantity of marking to do at home, instead of being able to mark in context, which is far more helpful to the children. The headteacher has discussed her problems with Miss Brown and has persuaded her to agree to try a group approach within a subject, for part of each day next term. She has explained a way of introducing this and has promised to help by taking some of the groups herself. Miss Brown is not looking forward to this but has agreed to try. Whereas Miss Brown would not take advice or help from her colleagues, she is prepared to accept both from the headteacher.

The head hopes that having made one step forward towards moving into the new school, each teacher, in the Summer term, will feel confident enough to make a further change. The staff are also attending a course at the local teachers' centre on preparation for teaching in the open plan school which includes topics such as cooperative teaching, team teaching, organization and record-keeping. Visits to existing open plan schools have also been arranged. When these take place in school hours the head tries to release two teachers at a time. If she and the part-time teacher each take over a class this is possible.

The head now turns her attention to preparing her managers and parents for the changes to come. They will inevitably measure the new school against their own experience otherwise. She has already been asked, 'Isn't this a step back? Old village schools had to have two classes in one room and it didn't always work very well.' Suspicions about motives for building in this way have also been voiced. 'Are they cheaper to build?' is another question often asked. These questions must be answered and correct information must be given. Next term, the head has decided, she must talk to the parent and the easiest way is to have evening meetings when both parents are available. She wants to talk about open plan schools and she is aware that she will have to justify new forms of organization. Year groups have always stayed together before and she knows that when some of each year group is grouped with younger children, some parents will see this as a lack of promotion and will want to know why Mary or John or Willie hasn't been moved up with others of his age. Vertical grouping will also have to be explained and justified, as will other innovations. She has material for several meetings. She has decided to send out a circular letter early in the new year suggesting dates, times, and topics for a series of three meetings in the Spring term. These could well be followed in the Summer term by sessions on practical maths, environmental studies and creative activities. Having by these means initiated parents' meetings by invitation, she hopes the interest in the new school will continue and that parents will want to be involved with all sorts of school activities.

References

GOLDBERG, M., JUSTMAN, J., PASSOE, A. M., MAGE, G. (1961). *The Effects of Ability Grouping* Lincoln: Horace Mann Lincoln Institute

4 Organization in purpose-built schools

The infant school

Activities usually provided in infant schools

1 Make believe: Home play
Large block construction
Railway lines
Garage etc
Dressing up
2 Basic: Wood, sand and water experiment
3 Creative activities: Art and craft
4 Maths/science: Practical work
Written work
Work cards
Reference books
5 Cookery:
6 Reading/writing: Enquiry and relaxation
Written work – personal and project
7 Music: Experiment and performance
8 PE: Movement and physical skills
9 Stories/RE/discussion/drama

10 Display: Central of work
11 Audio-visual: TV, radio, tape recorders (reel to reel and cassette)
Record player
Film strip projector and screen

Resources

1 Make believe: (a) bed, table, chairs, dresser, cooker, sink-unit, carpet
(b) dolls, clothes, bed, washing facilities
(c) crockery, cutlery, cleaning tools, cooking utensils
(d) bowl, bucket
(e) large blocks or multi-purpose units

		(f) trucks, trolleys, cars, garage, railway lines etc
		(g) dressing up – clothes and trolley
2	Basic:	Sand and water trays, woodwork bench
3	Creative:	Clay bin, easels, large worktops, plastic sheeting
		Papers various, brushes, glues, scissors, materials
		Storage for paper, materials, half-finished and completed work
4	Maths/science:	Worktop for practical work – storage under
		Worktop for recording and desk work
		Measures for length, weight, capacity, time, money and storage
		Apparatus for sorting, classifying, ordering etc and storage
		Work cards and reference book storage
		Display space
		Keeping pets
		Displays of scientific/natural materials
		Sink unit
5	Cooking:	Cooker, access to sink-unit, storage of utensils and materials
		Recipes and instructions – display
6	Reading/writing:	Book storage and display
		Room to use books
		Chairs, tables, pouffes, cushions, carpet
		Writing papers and tools – storage and worktop
		Storage of sources of stimuli – sensory
		Display space
7	Music:	Experiment – instruments – storage trolley
		Space in which to use these
		Singing and movement
8	PE:	Room in which to work
		Storage of apparatus, equipment and clothes
9	Stories/RE/discussion/drama:	Carpeted area, variety of seating
		Chair for teacher
		Space for drama
10	Display:	Wall and worktop space
		Wall display from floor to ceiling where possible
11	Audio-visual:	Adequate provision of power points and aerials
		Storage for expensive equipment

Having identified the activities usually provided and the resources necessary for each, the next step is to decide where the activities are to be placed. Most architects provide a layout plan of movable furniture indicating a possible distribution. This only suggests how the prescribed amount of furniture will fit into the overall area. It does not indicate that this is either the best or only method of distribution. It is the people who ultimately use the building who decide where the furniture is to go. It is quite possible, and in fact happens, that where there are two identical units provided in a school, the facilities in each are quite differently arranged, depending on the needs, ideas, interests and priorities of the people using them.

A useful step in deciding where to put things is to make a scale plan of the unit together with cut-out outlines of pieces of furniture also to scale. The teachers who are to use the unit can then discuss its possibilities, and try out the furniture in different positions. In this way they can decide together where each teacher is to be based, and what the emphasis of each area is to be. They can agree where to locate activities and resources, and decide where practical work is to take place and where the quieter and more studious pursuits can operate. Figure 13 (opposite) indicates the results of one such exercise.

This school is intended to accommodate 240 pupils in two identical units, each of which houses 120 children with their teachers. In addition a shared reference area, a shared enclosable room, a hall, a kitchen and an administrative block including staff accommodation are provided. There is also an internal courtyard.

This plan shows one entire unit for 120 children with table and chair provision for approximately 60 per cent of the children excluding worktop and stools. Various shapes of tables are available. Some of the worktop area has recessed shelving under to allow for storage of apparatus, whilst other worktops provide storage for trolleys (indicated by dotted outline). Some book shelving over worktops and elswhere is also available. Most of the other walls are hessian covered and provide display space.

. Trolley provision also gives variety of storage. Some are tray trolleys providing storage of personal belongings for each child; some have mixed shelving and tray-storage facilities. There are three trolleys which give low-level cupboard storage and which have high backs with display panels on one side and blackboard on the other. There is a general-purpose trolley with a variety of different-sized trays for use in the practical area and a dressing-up trolley located in one of the carpeted bays. Also provided are three physical education trolleys with storage for plimsolls. Three deep storage bins are also available.

In the practical area a trough sink gives facilities for water play and there are also a sand tray, a clay table and a woodwork bench. In the practical bay a sink is set into the worktop and a small cooker has also been provided.

The cloakroom and lavatory facilities are located centrally and near to a door leading to outside play areas. The shaded portions indicate cloaks storage with high-level cupboard storage over. These cupboards are intended for the use of the teacher. There is also a drinking fountain.

The question of where to place the children arises. Some people might choose to place the younger children in one unit and the older ones in the

Figure 13

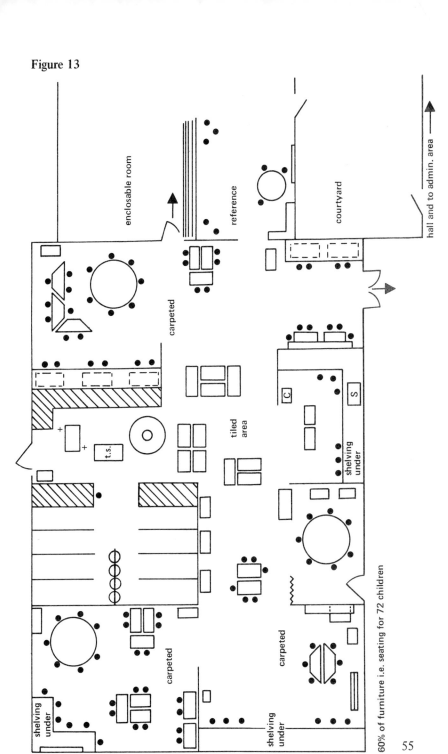

enclosable room

reference

carpeted

courtyard

hall and to admin. area

tiled
area

t.s.

shelving
under

C

S

shelving
under

carpeted

carpeted

shelving
under

shelving
under

60% of furniture i.e. seating for 72 children

55

Figure 14

1 Unit 1 Younger children and entrants

Unit 2 Older children

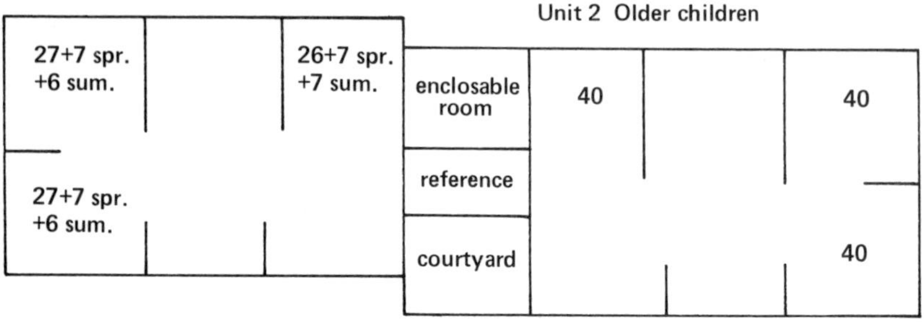

27+7 spr. +6 sum.		26+7 spr. +7 sum.	enclosable room	40		40
			reference			
27+7 spr. +6 sum.			courtyard			40

2 Unit 1 Vertical group

Unit 2 Vertical group

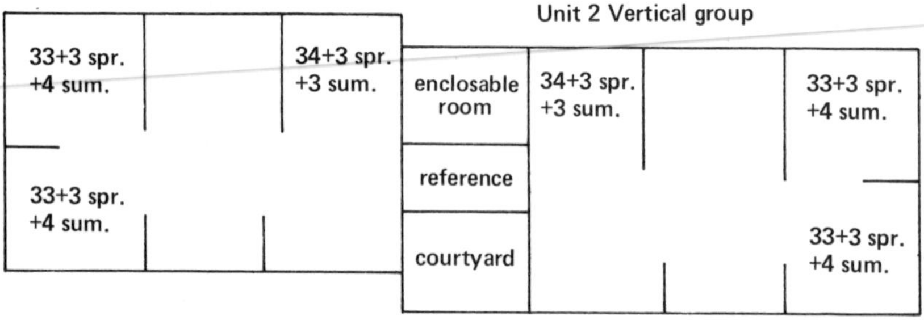

33+3 spr. +4 sum.		34+3 spr. +3 sum.	enclosable room	34+3 spr. +3 sum.		33+3 spr. +4 sum.
			reference			
33+3 spr. +4 sum.			courtyard			33+3 spr. +4 sum.

3 Unit 1 Transitional vertical group

Unit 2 Transitional vertical group

30+5 spr. +5 sum.		40 older	enclosable room	40 older		30+5 spr. +5 sum.
			reference			
30+5 spr. +5 sum.			courtyard			30+5 spr. +5 sum.

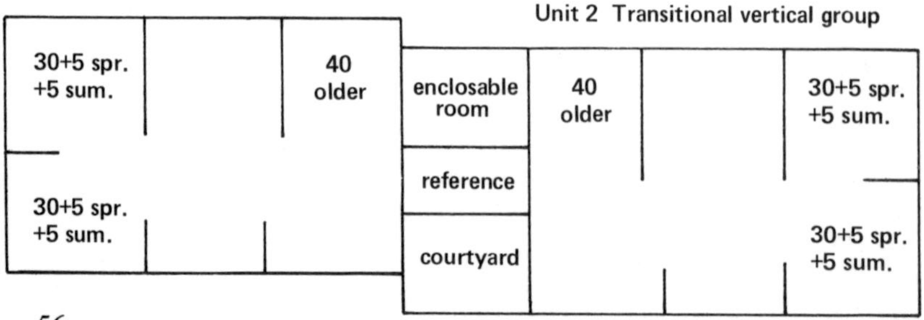

other. It is likely that the unit containing the older children would have its full complement for the whole of the school year whilst the other has smaller groups initially which build up with termly intake to 120 in the Summer term. Others might feel that to have 120 in one unit for the whole year produces an unnecessary strain on its occupants, staff and children alike. They might choose to vertically group throughout and have identical numbers in the first term, with identical intake numbers in each unit in the Spring and Summer terms. Another alternative might be to have transitional vertical groups in two of the home bases in each unit which could accommodate intake numbers in the Spring and Summer terms, with a third older and full-strength group whose number remains static throughout the year in the third home base.

It is hoped that the school would be staffed by a headteacher and seven full-time assistants. The seventh teacher could be used in a variety of ways depending on experience, interests, and expertise.

The three examples of organization suggested later are relevant whichever form of grouping is adopted.

Figure 15 (page 58) shows the approximate sizes of the various work spaces within the unit, and also shows where resources are to be found. Notice how trolleys may be grouped together in the art/craft area to provide large working surfaces. If these trolleys contain the materials necessary for the activity and are placed back to back, easy access to the materials is immediately possible. For example, if the four trolleys marked 'Collage' on the plan (each storing appropriate materials of different textures and colours on the shelves and different small items like braid, ribbons, string, buttons, beads and sequins) all face outward, without doors, everything necessary is to hand. Similarly the three trolleys designated 'Models' could contain different pieces of junk material, scissors, paste pots and brushes, sellotape, masking tape, and different kinds of covering materials. In this way, the children know where to find everything necessary for the activity and also where to put things back. The deep bins on casters provide storage for blocks, pieces of wood for woodwork and other bulky items, and can be trundled to wherever they are required.

Alternative forms of organization
A form of rotation is shown in Figure 16 (page 59) where, in order to become familiar with provision, children remain with their teacher in one area for the whole of one morning. After the mid-day break Group 1 moves to Group 3 home base and has the use of the 'make-believe' and art/craft facilities for the rest of the day. Similarly Group 3 'rotates' to the enclosable room and Group 2 moves into home base 1 to the English and reference areas. The following morning, after registration in the home bases, Group 1 will go with their teacher to home base 2 and the practical maths/science area, Group 2 will move to home base 3 and the art/craft area, and Group 3 will move into the English and reference areas.

Figure 15

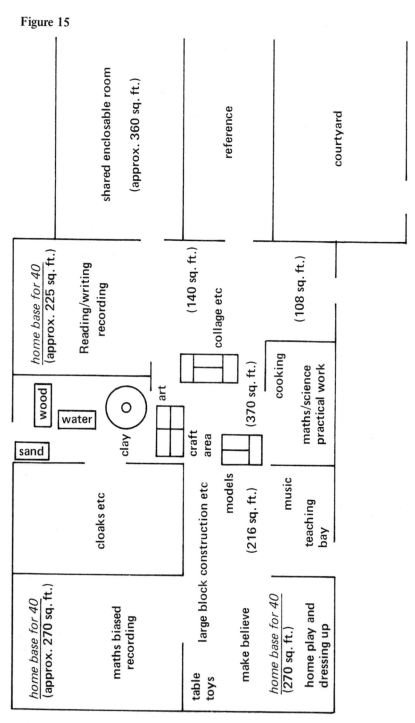

shared enclosable room
(approx. 360 sq. ft.)

reference

courtyard

home base for 40 (approx. 225 sq. ft.)

Reading/writing recording

(140 sq. ft.)

collage etc

(108 sq. ft.)

wood

water

clay

art

craft area

cooking

maths/science practical work

(370 sq. ft.)

sand

cloaks etc

large block construction etc

models

music

teaching bay

(216 sq. ft.)

home base for 40 (approx. 270 sq. ft.)

maths biased recording

table toys

make believe

home base for 40 (270 sq. ft.)

home play and dressing up

58

Figure 16

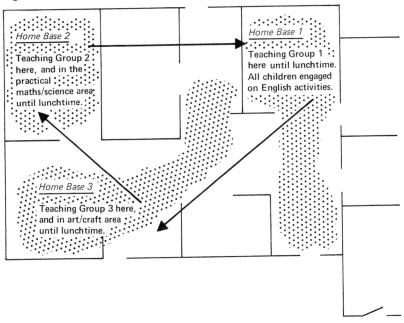

This practice will enable staff and children to find out where everything lives reasonably quickly. Some teachers may feel that they need a day in each area initially rather than a half day. As staff and children become familiar with the facilities they may wish to make their stay in each area shorter. It may be felt that from registration to break is long enough in any one area. However, in order to accommodate various work speeds and task involvements it may become necessary to allow teaching groups to mingle. For example a small group from Teaching Group 3 may be allowed to remain in the art/craft area to complete a task with which they are deeply involved, whilst the rest of the group moves on to home base 2 — maths. Similarly some children from Teaching Group 1 may have some recording to complete and may be left behind in home base 1 whilst the rest of the group moves into home base 3 — art/craft. When the various tasks are completed those left behind move on.

In its early stages this type of organization could be criticised in that it splits the day into subject areas and precludes true unity of learning. As teachers and children become familiar with the system, however, mingling of the three groups happens more frequently and the rigidity of rotation by class breaks down into more natural learning patterns.

Figure 17

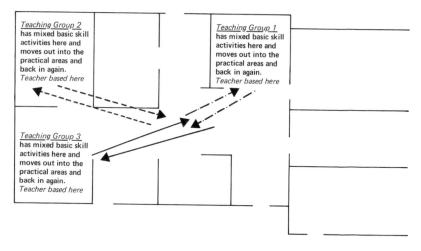

Teaching Group 2
has mixed basic skill
activities here and
moves out into the
practical areas and
back in again.
Teacher based here

Teaching Group 1
has mixed basic skill
activities here and
moves out into the
practical areas and
back in again.
Teacher based here

Teaching Group 3
has mixed basic skill
activities here and
moves out into the
practical areas and
back in again.
Teacher based here

Here each teaching group has a home base which is equipped for all basic skill activities. The children move out into the shared practical areas and back again into their home base, which in this case is _not_ shared with other groups. This type of organization can be criticised in that three sets of basic skill apparatus and equipment have to be provided, and there is, therefore, less money available for a greater variety of provision in other areas of learning.

It also provides less opportunity for children to mingle and possibly less opportunity for sharing of ideas. It also tends to mean that when one class is out of the unit for physical education or some other similar purpose, their home base remains empty, so that in this case the other classes do not benefit as much from their absence.

In Figure 18, after a 'together' session in the home base when planning of work may have been taking place, the children disperse throughout the unit. The teacher in home base 1 keeps a group of children with her in the home base for direct teaching. (The round tables in each home base have been designated as 'teaching tables'.) Six more have been given a group assignment in maths and two others have opted to do maths first. Three girls and five boys have gone to the make-believe/construction

Figure 18   Group 1 home base: reading/writing area

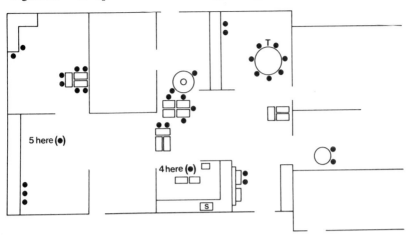

area. Four have a cooking assignment, under the supervision of the ancillary, while eight others have chosen to do some form of art. Six others have opted to do some form of English.

'Together' sessions usually happen at the beginning and end of the day, by mutual consent. They can also happen at the end of the morning or beginning of the afternoon session. The children may need these 'together' times more frequently initially, until they become used to the situation. Together times can include such activities as registration, planning the day's (or half day's) work, discussing a 'theme' and deciding who is to do what, story-time, religious education, or simply assessment of one another's work. Time spent together will vary from class to class, and from day to day. Should a class group need to come together at some other time during the day then the enclosable room provides an opportunity to do so.

The teacher in home base 2 maths area (see Figure 19) also keeps a group for direct teaching. In this case another group of six children have been given an English assignment, while five others have opted to do reading/writing first. Four children have remained in the home base to do maths whilst two others have gone to work in the practical maths/science area, to complete some work begun earlier. Four girls and three boys have

Figure 19   Group 2 home base: maths biased area

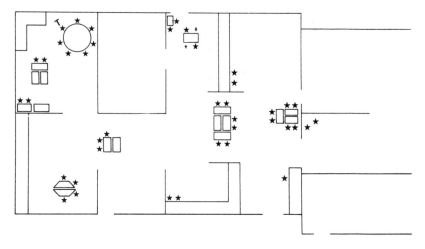

gone to the make-believe/construction area. Six others have an art/craft assignment and four are engaged in sand and wood work.

In home base 3 (Figure 20) the teacher has kept a group for direct teaching and five other children will remain in the make-believe area. Four children are working on a group assignment in maths and six others have also opted to be in the maths area. Three others are engaged in water play and two are finishing models in the art area whilst three more are finishing some practical maths/science work. Eleven children have chosen to do some kind of English activity — four of whom have a definite assignment.

In Figure 21 all three groups are shown in position distributed throughout the entire unit. In each case the group at the teaching table may be receiving direct teaching in any of the basic skills, or may be discussing a project or theme with their teachers. The teacher may also take this opportunity to check on work done, or suggest how work can develop.

For the purpose of this exercise let us suppose that the teacher in home base 2 — maths area has kept a group of pre-readers with her to discuss a picture connected with the reading scheme. She may be assessing the previous experience of the children in the group, their understanding of the situation and their language development, whilst introducing the words

Figure 20   Group 3 home base: make believe/home play area

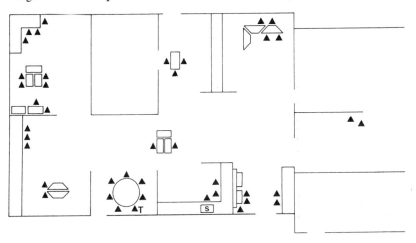

needed by the children for future involvement in the reading scheme. She might then give them an assignment such as finding five objects in the unit which are red and drawing them, after which they might choose what they would like to do until playtime. Having dismissed this group the teacher (who has planned her day previously) will make her way through the unit stopping to comment on work and activities and giving help and encouragement where needed. As she moves through the unit she can collect those children whom she wishes to teach next: they will take their trays and any apparatus needed to the teaching table ready for her return. She then returns to her home base where she gives some direct teaching in some aspect of mathematics, following this with a practice to consolidate her teaching. She then hears these individuals read one by one, after which she again makes her way through the unit. This time she collects the six children who are engaged on the English assignment and they take their work back to the home base. Here she checks the work they have been doing, discusses it and makes suggestions about how it might continue. She may then give this group some direct teaching in maths and set practice work for them to do later in the day. After break this teacher and her entire group prepare for PE and go to the hall.

Meanwhile the teachers in the other home bases have also released

Figure 21

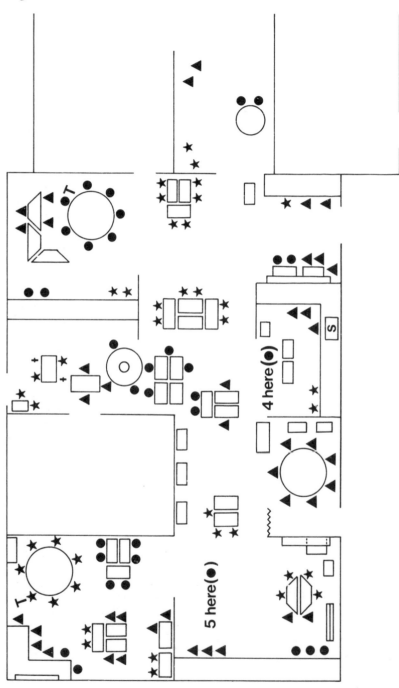

children and collected new groups. Other children too will have finished one activity and moved on to another. Places will, therefore, have been vacated in various parts of the unit into which other children can move. There is no specific time for these changes to occur. Each teaching group will collect and disperse as the need arises. Similarly children move when they finish the activity on which they have been engaged.

Figure 22 indicates a possible redistribution of the children. The three original teaching groups have been disbanded and have gone about various tasks. Three children from Teaching Group 1 (circle) have gone to the trolleys in the make-believe/construction area and three others have gone to paint. A fresh group has been gathered by the teacher from the maths area and the art area. The children from Teaching Group 2 (star) have gone also – two to practial maths, two to the reference area, one to paint and one to write. A new Teaching Group 2 has been collected from the reference and home-play areas. The six children from Teaching Group 3 (triangle) have also dispersed. Four have gone to maths with an assignment from the teacher and the other two have gone to the models table. The new Teaching Group 3 has been formed by withdrawing six children from the maths areas.

Many of the other children have also moved whilst some have not yet completed their original tasks and are still *in situ*. Some children who have been engaged on practical activities such as cooking, wookwork, model making and maths/science have gone to record what they have been doing either graphically or in writing. Others who have been writing have gone to make things to illustrate their writing, or have simply felt a need to relax and have gone to the craft or make-believe areas. Some have gone to the reference area to look up information about something they are making, and others have gone to read for pleasure or to practise reading techniques. One group who were building a boat with blocks and whose play had deteriorated and become noisy and overactive, disturbing others near at hand, have been sent by their teacher to record the different shapes used in their construction.

Changes of activity have been undertaken for a variety of reasons. Some follow on naturally one from another and show a definite relationship and pattern of work. Others seem to be unrelated but may not be. Some are undertaken voluntarily whilst others are teacher directed.

To ensure that the system does not break down, preparation and good organization are essential. There should also be plenty of alternative activities in each area, so that as little frustration as possible occurs.

It is not necessary for children to be seated for every activity. Maths equipment such as Dienes logiblocks, or activities involving large graphic recordings, group games in the English area such as Lotto and dominoes, and large pieces of collage or frieze work are probably better accommodated on the floor.

This type of organization relates most closely to the flexible way of working described in Chapter 2.

Figure 22

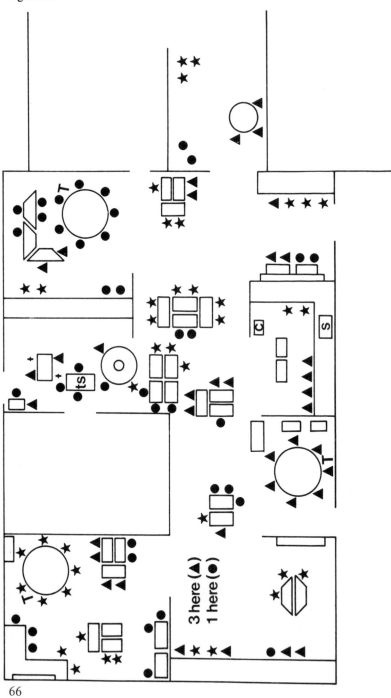

3 here (▲)
1 here (●)

Figure 23   Timetable for hall and enclosable room

	MONDAY							
	1	2	3	4	5	6	7	8
1	H					enclosable room pm		
2		H						
3			H					
4					H			
5	enclosable room am					H		
6							H	

	TUESDAY							
	1	2	3	4	5	6	7	8
1	enclosable room am						H	
2								H
3		H						
4				H				
5						H	enclosable room pm	
6						H		

	WEDNESDAY							
	1	2	3	4	5	6	7	8
1	enclosable room am			H				
2			H					
3						H		
4						H		
5	H			enclosable room pm				
6			H					

	THURSDAY							
	1	2	3	4	5	6	7	8
1							H	
2		H		enclosable room pm				
3			H					
4	enclosable room am				H			
5						H		
6							H	

	FRIDAY							
	1	2	3	4	5	6	7	8
1	enclosable room am			H				
2					H			
3						H		
4	H					enclosable room pm		
5			H					
6			H					

30 min. period in hall each day

Hall also used for assemblies; dining.

Last period each day, available to each unit or class in turn.

The hall timetable shown here is one of many possibilities. In this version classes in each unit have consecutive periods allocated, so that within the unit some flexibility is possible, and teachers could exchange times or join forces if necessary.

First and last periods each day are free and could be available to either unit as required. Alternatively if the hall were required for a longer period for meals, the fourth and fifth periods could be made free and the first and last periods allocated for PE instead.

Each teaching group has five hall periods allocated during the week and a different time has been allocated each day. Normally PE might take place out of doors on two days and in the hall on the other three days. This would make two periods in the hall available to each class for other activities. In inclement weather the hall period should be used for some form of movement.

The enclosable room has also been timetabled in such a way that it is available to each unit in turn, for the whole of a morning or afternoon session, and alternates as far as possible with the hall provision. No specific allocation has been made to any class which gives complete flexibility within each unit.

Availability of the hall and enclosable room in this way means that for the majority of each day there need never be more than two classes in either unit.

Cooperation
It is envisaged that the teachers within the unit will wish to agree schemes of work and syllabuses, projects and themes. Within this framework each teacher would be responsible for pastoral care, planning and recording of basic skill work for her own teaching group, and for her group's contribution to cooperative work.

Recording requires either that time must be set aside for checking each individual's output, or that teachers agree to pool information about what they observe throughout the unit. Both may be thought necessary.

Use of space
Flexibility in the implementation of the hall timetable can be achieved by consultation between staff members and by mutual agreement.

Similarly use of the enclosable room which is equipped for TV and visual aids can be arranged by mutual agreement. It could be that one teaching group from a unit was using the hall, another group the enclosable room, leaving the rest of the unit available for the exclusive use of the remaining teaching group, for a short period.

The small teaching bay, if fitted with curtains and an electric point, could be utilized by a small group with a slide projector, or for experimental music. Again this would be by arrangement.

Quiet times
These will probably need to be agreed by all teachers in the unit. However, most traditional classes begin and end the day with such a period.

The first school: 5–9 years of age
It has already been stated that when he enters school the young entrant needs to come into a welcoming and secure situation, where he can make a good relationship with his teacher and the other children in his group. He needs to find all sorts of interesting things which will stimulate thought, action and language. Gradually as he matures the young child widens his horizons and makes relationships with other adults and other children within the school. Initially the child is very much an individual and even in the play situation may work on his own, alongside but not with other children. As he grows older he begins to take part in shared activities but still needs the support of adults. Round about the age of nine he feels able to assert his independence and begins to reject the support of the adult and turns instead to the children in his peer group.

As entrants children usually exhibit very short periods of concentration and sustained activity although this varies from child to child. As they mature the periods of concentration lengthen and work speeds accelerate.

Given a daily opportunity for practising, consolidating and developing skills, they acquire greater facility in the use of tools and improved techniques in all aspects of development – social, emotional, intellectual, physical and so on. Whether he is five or nine years of age, development of the whole person is essential. Throughout this period children become increasingly self-sufficient and can, towards the age of nine, to some extent organize their own individual group or class activities whilst the teacher remains unobtrusively in control and ready to supply help, guidance and support whenever necessary.

It seems appropriate, therefore, in view of this gradual development, to use an extension of infant methods up to the age of nine, involving the use of resources, materials and equipment, books and tools of increasing sophistication, at more sophisticated levels as the need arises. This would ensure progression and continuity and also provide the necessary increase in pace and depth of the child's learning processes. Whether a child is five or nine he should be acquiring new knowledge based on previous experience. Recognition of the differing developmental needs of eac^1 individual, whatever the level of his ability, is of paramount importance.

Grouping the children
A first school built to accommodate 240 children in two identical units could be arranged in a variety of ways. Two obvious alternatives would be:

1   to arrange the school 'end-on' with the younger children in one unit and the older children in the other.
2   to arrange the school in two parallel units with full age range 5–9 years in each unit.

Within these two main systems a variety of procedures is possible:

1   (i)   the younger unit could be vertically grouped with children of 5–7 in three class groups, and with two transitional groups in the other unit with the very oldest children in a group by themselves.
    (ii) two transitional groups accommodating the youngest children and entrants with a separate group containing the oldest infants in unit 1 and 2 with three separate older groups keeping as much as possible to year groups in unit 2.
2   (i)   both units with three classes fully vertically grouped (5–9 years).
    (ii) both units with one class of mixed five and six year olds, one class containing some six year olds, all the sevens and some eight year olds, and one class of mixed eight and nine year olds.

There are many other alternatives.

Figure 24

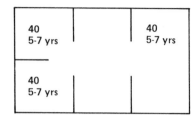

1 Unit 1 5-7

| 40
5-7 yrs | | 40
5-7 yrs |
| 40
5-7 yrs | | |

Unit 2 7-9

| 40
7+8 yrs | | 40
7+8 yrs |
| | | 40
oldest
mostly 9 yrs |

1 Unit 1 5-7

| 40
5+6 yrs | | 40
oldest
6 yrs
and
youngest
7 yrs |
| 40
5+6 yrs | | |

Unit 2 7-9

| 40
7+8 yrs | | 40
8+9 yrs |
| | | 40 oldest
children
mostly 9 yrs |

2 Unit 1 5-9

| 40
5-9 yrs | | 40
5-9 yrs |
| 40
5-9 yrs | | |

Unit 2 5-9

| 40
5-9 yrs | | 40
5-9 yrs |
| | | 40
5-9 yrs |

2 Unit 1 5-9

| 40
5+6 yrs | | 40
8+9 yrs |
| 40
6,7,8 yrs | | |

Unit 2 5-9

| 40
8+9 yrs | | 40
5+6 yrs |
| | | 40
6,7+8 yrs |

70

The junior school

Resources

Years 1 and 2

1 Dressing up facilities: Space to work
2 Creative activities: Basic materials, woodwork bench, art/craft materials as for infants
3 Maths/science: Sand and water facilities for capacity work
Otherwise materials as for infants, but more sophisticated apparatus and equipment
4 Cooking: As for infants
5 Language: As for infants
Book provision within a library area where possible
6 Music: As for infants
7 PE: As for infants
More sophisticated equipment
Opportunities for swimming
8 Oral work with the teacher: Carpeted area, variety of seating
9 Display: As for infants
Need for flexible arrangements
10 Audio-visual: As for infants, plus remedial equipment (e.g. Language Master, Synchrofax, typewriter)
Film projector

Years 3 and 4

As for years 1 and 2, but add the following:
Creative: Kiln
Clay storage and shelving
Metalwork facilities (introductory, e.g. enamelling, simple soldering)
Maths/science: More advanced equipment, possibly in greater quantity
Music: Instruments of more sophistication
PE: More games equipment

A junior school designed to accommodate 240 children might also be designed in two identical units with other shared facilities: the units would again house 120 children with their teachers. Similarly it is hoped that the school would be staffed by a headteacher and seven full-time assistants with an appropriate provision of ancillary staff.

The seventh teacher in this case may have been specially trained in remedial/slow-learner work and might be employed in each unit for half-days or half-sessions alternately, withdrawing children for short periods from each class to give help where it is required. Alternatively this teacher might be given responsibility for a particular group of children of mixed ability drawn from the three classes for half of each day, thus effectively reducing the numbers in each class for 50 per cent of the time. Or this teacher might be employed generally throughout each unit in turn giving help where it is needed. The seventh teacher might on the other hand be the deputy head whose responsibility it is to coordinate work in both units. There are a number of possibilities depending on the experience, expertise and interests of the person concerned.

Figure 25   3 class junior unit, for third and fourth year juniors

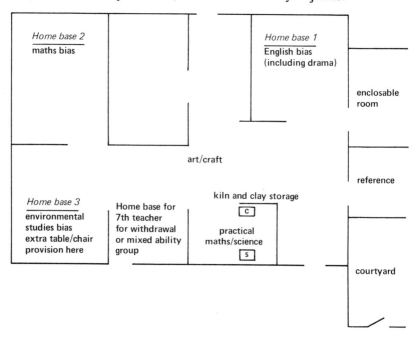

This plan indicates where the seventh teacher might be positioned in the unit. It also shows a redistribution of some of the facilities appropriate for older juniors. For example whilst there are still dressing-up facilities these are now located in the English area, and their use will have progressed from the spontaneous dramatic play of the young child to the making up, writing and acting of plays — a much more sophisticated group activity, which if necessary can spill over into the enclosable room. Similarly the emphasis in home base 3 has changed from 'make-believe' to the study of the actual environment, including history, geography and natural science.

Some older juniors will have developed considerably intellectually. They will have progressed beyond sensory experience and use of concrete materials, and will be beginning to work with images, abstracting what they require from all kinds of remembered previous experience. Their periods of concentration and involvement with tasks will be longer-lasting. Some, of course, will still need recourse to concrete materials, and some will be able to work with symbols for part of the time but, not being completely confident, will need opportunity to revert to concrete materials from time to time. It could be expected, however, that the degree of movement in the unit might be less and that there might be a greater demand for sedentary occupations. A 70 per cent seating provision might be more appropriate for a third and fourth year junior unit.

Similarly craft skills will have developed tremendously and the older junior is capable of precise and delicate work. Hence the provision of a kiln, clay storage and shelving in the art/craft area, and of simple heating equipment in the practical area for various kinds of craft activities.

Basic organization in this unit can follow any of the three patterns suggested for the infant unit, i.e. (a) rotation (see Figure 16 page 59), (b) basic skills within the home base with shared use of practical areas (see Figure 17 page 60), or (c) the situation where all three (or four) class groups are distributed throughout the unit sharing all the facilities simultaneously (see Figure 21 page 64). Each class can work separately, or there can be cooperation between two or all of the groups.

Grouping the children can again involve vertical grouping, transitional vertical grouping, year groups or a combination of these. If the school were double the size and two identical units were provided for third and fourth year juniors it is still possible for the children in the two units to be grouped quite differently from one another, according to the needs of the children and/or staff operating within them.

The enclosable room
A case could be made for the provision of an extra enclosable room of about 360—420 sq. ft. in the junior school. Third and fourth year juniors may need such a space more often, which could result in younger children being deprived of a percentage of their share of this provision for quiet and noisy activities.

Many primary schools teach French to their third and fourth year juniors and most of the schools teaching French use a class teaching approach involving equipment such as tape-recorders and projectors. It is desirable to provide a daily lesson for each class involved in learning French. In a school with a third and fourth year unit of three class groups the enclosable room would need to be used for fifteen periods each week for French alone, leaving only five-eighths of the total time available for use in other ways and by other classes.

Greater use is often made by older juniors of television programmes, either as a stimulus for integrated work in the unit, or as part of a programme devised by the teachers, and a follow-up of an interest begun elsewhere. Many schools nowadays are selective in their use of television programmes, and include only those items which fit in to planned programmes of work. However, these need careful timetabling if they are to be used to greatest advantage. It is perhaps even more necessary in the 'open-plan' school to be selective about use of television, so that the enclosable room is available for other activities.

Other items of equipment such as overhead projectors used, perhaps, to introduce a class to a particular aspect of geography in a local studies project, also need the seclusion provided by the enclosable room. Indeed the enclosable room would provide the most suitable venue for introduction of new material in any aspect of the curriculum, necessitating a class approach.

Music, which at upper junior level will have moved from the experimental stage to a greater emphasis on performance may very well entail an increased use of the enclosable room both for vocal and instrumental music either for small or class groups.

The seventh teacher might need to withdraw groups from the busy atmosphere of the unit for some specific skill instruction. The enclosable room might well provide the ideal place for short-term activities for which removal from distraction is necessary.

It is also probably true to say that fewer junior teachers than infant teachers have been used to cooperative teaching situations, and that they, therefore, need more opportunity to withdraw into an enclosable room when first involved in an 'open-plan' school.

It is interesting to note how these problems are surmounted where only one enclosable room has been provided. Small rooms designated for other uses such as the deputy head's room, the medical room, the staffroom and even the head's room may be utilized for small group work in some schools and free periods in the hall are 'snapped up' for class activities. Provision of a second enclosable room would probably be beneficial where third and fourth year juniors are concerned if only for purposes of timetabling. Timetabling of spaces such as these becomes more complicated, it seems, as children grow older. There will have been a gradual development away from 'unity of learning' as seen in the infant department where the young child does not differentiate between subjects, but simply 'learns', towards a definition of 'areas of study', and even, in some cases, of single subjects, e.g. French in the upper junior department. Even so shared areas, such as the units in which individual and group activities predominate, need not be timetabled. It is those spaces where class activities happen which need to be timetabled. If, as has been suggested above, upper juniors need the enclosable room for a greater variety of activities, timetabling will be more complicated.

5 A larger junior school

Previous chapters have described the work in schools which are organized in two- or three-teacher units. Some schools are designed to an even more 'open' concept, with four or even more teachers working with large numbers of children in an open space. This chapter considers the organization of a two-form entry junior school with about 320 children on roll.

Figure 26

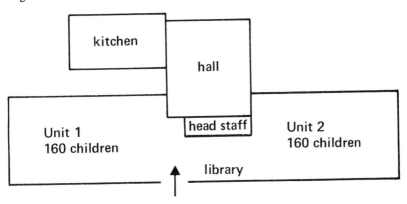

Figure 26 shows the layout of the school, with 160 children in each of the two wings. On a 1:40 teacher: pupil ratio, four teachers would work in each unit with the children (four classes in a traditional school with classrooms). In recent years there has been a gradual move to better ratios, and many authorities would be able to allocate five teachers to each unit in this school. This gives an overall ratio of eleven staff (including the headteacher) to 320 children, just under a 1:30 ratio and well within the figures for primary school staffing which most authorities allocate.

The work of a modern open plan school makes great demands on teachers, and many would argue for a more generous staffing for these schools than for the traditional schools with classrooms. The argument is based on the pressures to which teachers are subject when the school is trying to keep every child at full stretch according to his needs and abilities. But many schools of older design have the same educational ideals about the individual development of children, and it is doubtful if the new schools can claim especially generous staffing. On the other hand, it is true that a box classroom seating rows of children in a 'talk and chalk' situation can be, and often is, overcrowded, i.e. with more than forty children. Indeed, early elementary schools often sat hundreds of children in rows facing the one teacher, and it is true that a lecturer today can deliver his message to hundreds of students in the lecture theatre (and to millions watching him on the television screen). But a new open plan school cannot for long have large numbers of children seated in rows to receive the instruction; the work must be individual, and therefore there must be a certain amount of movement and 'freedom' to follow individual interests and schemes of work. It follows that such a school should not be overcrowded. However, it does seem that economic stringencies may well force local authorities at times to pack more and more children into a school, and whereas an average-sized class box could as well seat forty as thirty, this sort of pressure is intolerable in an open school. Ideally, the school discussed in this chapter should have five teachers in each unit, plus at least one supernumerary teacher used, perhaps, for remedial work, or some other kind of skilled work, in both units. Be that as it may, for the purposes of this chapter, let us assume that the ratio is about 1:30 overall, and that the Education Office is cooperating by refusing to allow the total numbers in the school to exceed 320.

The situation then is that the five teachers will work together in each unit or department. The detailed organization of such a large team is of great importance: too tight a control of the teaching spaces and the timetable will result in a rigid, formal system which will minimize the advantages of the building; but too free an organization could produce a situation where children may lack security and where they may waste their time. Therefore, careful planning of the three most important resources — teaching strength, time and space — must retain the freedom and efficiency that have evolved from the best of modern methods.

In Figure 27, one of the units for 160 children is shown in detail. In all probability, most headteachers would halve the school into upper and lower juniors, and the unit shown could be for either the seven and eight year olds or the nines and tens.

The total area of the teaching space is about 3200 square feet, and it includes a large activity or general-purpose practical area (about 2300 sq. ft.). This large space contains a 'wet area' with sinks, storage for art/craft work, and the like. There are also three bays. Two enclosable spaces of differing sizes are available, each of them with folding doors which allow the rooms to be opened onto the general area. There is

Figure 27 Unit for 160 children

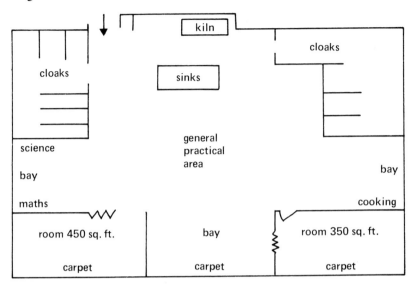

furniture (seats and tables) for about 110 children (70 per cent) and storage trays for the children's personal use. Fitted cupboards, sinks, shelving and storage are adequate. Mobile storage units would be an important part of this school's equipment. One of the bays contains an electric cooker, and there is a kiln and damp cupboard for clay work in the wet area. A television set is installed in the larger of the two enclosable rooms, and this room is reasonably soundproof. The two rooms and one of the bays are carpeted, but the general activity area and two of the bays have floor surfaces which will not be damaged by water. Thus, children's art and craft activities need not be confined to the small area by the sinks. Indeed, the increasing use of carpeted floors in new primary schools has sometimes led to a reduction in the amount of space which could be used for messy activities.

Each teacher is responsible for a group of about thirty-two children, but the concept of a 'class' in the traditional sense has to be modified. In the first instance, there are only two rooms large enough to accommodate a class of over thirty children. As there will be times in every day when the teacher needs to bring his own group together, the first problem is to organize space for the 'together times' (e.g. registration, story-telling, class discussion, preparing new work etc).

It is tempting to divide the total space into five 'classrooms', one in each enclosable room and three in the open area. The main disadvantage is that the practical area would not be easily available for children based in

the two rooms. A complex 'rotating' timetable would be required so that all children have access during the week to the wet area, cooker, television set and so on. Another disadvantage is that the concept of 'one teacher — one class' (as in a class box) is too static for this building. An alternative is required which is both flexible and easy to organize.

In the lower junior department, it may be necessary to base the work mainly in classes for a time. The incoming seven year olds may particularly need the security at first of their own group space. They may be especially bewildered if they have come from a more formal infant school where the teaching has been confined to rooms. For them, the large open spaces could be overwhelming, so the teachers may wish to organize class spaces where they can give the security that the young children need.

Figure 28

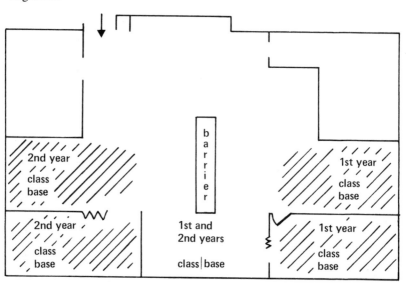

Figure 28 shows the unit halved by a barrier made from mobile storage cupboards and high sheets of corrugated cardboard. Each year group has half of the total teaching space and has access to an enclosable room, an activity space and the wet area. The first year children are given the security of their 'own' space with their own teacher, and they will not be bewildered by being among the large number of children throughout the whole unit. There is also a class of mixed first and second year children sharing one space: the first year children here could be the more mature ones who may have had longer at school.

In effect, this temporary arrangement fulfils the aim of giving security to the new entrants. It also means that the teachers work as class teachers in the traditional sense, i.e. one teacher with his 'own' group of about thirty children for most of the day. As the children settle in, there could be some movement so that the teachers of the first year classes cooperate and evolve some methods of sharing the work for the whole of the year group. Thus the larger team of five teachers is broken down into two smaller teams based on year groups, and this may make for easier organization at the beginning of the school year.

However, it must be emphasized that this system is a temporary expedient designed to give young children more security in the first instance. Indeed, children who have already experienced the flexible methods of an open plan infant school will have far less need to be enclosed in rooms and behind barriers. After only a short time, during which they establish relationships in the unit and learn the possibilities of the building, they could easily be absorbed into the main stream of the department, working alongside their older colleagues. The family grouping situation which the unit offers is well known to many teachers and need not impose insoluble problems.

Another possible organization of the lower school department would be to reserve the smaller enclosable room for a special class of slower learners. There are arguments for and against the isolation of slower learners in this way, and this will be considered in a later chapter.

Many readers will surely argue that the erection of barriers in open spaces and the class teaching of children in fixed areas is against the spirit of the kind of learning which the new schools were designed to encourage. Certainly, the children's individual learning could not be effectively organized if a teaching department held the pupils in class units for a long period. Indeed, the only result would be to have the worst of the class box situation without any of the advantages of the new building with its specialized areas and equipment. The arrangement suggested in Figure 28 is similar to several that are seen in lower school departments at the very beginning of the academic year, and the system is quickly abandoned after the new children have come to feel at home. Much will depend upon such circumstances as the experience of the teachers, the backgrounds of the children and their education in infant school, and the limits imposed by the design of the building.

The erection of temporary barriers, screens and walls raises an important aspect of school design. For many teachers, the school should be so planned that flexible allocation of space may be quickly made. Thus, rooms for class teaching at the beginning of the school year or at odd times during any week should be available by opening or closing partitions. The partition should be so flexible that class, group and individual learning can take place easily in spaces of differing size and scope. But a building has to have its internal retaining walls, so no school can be 100 per cent flexible. It is not possible for a building to have all the internal walls so constructed that they can be immediately rearranged to make new spaces.

For this reason, there has to be a continual compromise between the ideals of modern teaching and the constraints created by the building. Nevertheless, the new buildings can afford far more possibilities for flexible teaching than the old schools with classrooms, and the erection of temporary barriers is not necessarily a retrograde step in a new situation. Many teachers would soon find the allocation of class spaces in an open plan school to be most unsatisfactory, and they would wish to move on to the child-centred and learning-centred approaches now to be considered.

The arrangement in Figure 29 shows the five teachers in either the lower or upper junior department with their 'own' class groups for 'together time'. Most teachers will wish to meet their children at the beginning and end of the school day, and also probably just before and after the break for lunch.

Figure 29

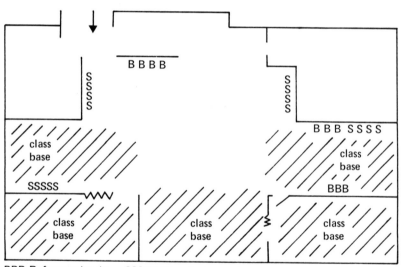

BBB Reference books   SSS Children's storage trays

During the short spells with their teacher, the children in the carpeted bay will probably sit on the floor or on some form of low seating (fixed padded bench seating or stools). In the two rooms the children could have chairs, but they need not necessarily be sitting at tables. For discussion or story work, many teachers would prefer the children to sit in a group, some on the carpeted floors, some on chairs, stools or cushions. The children will also need chairs or stools in the two bays which are not carpeted. The morning 'together time' need be of only very short duration: children and teacher will deal with registration, collect dinner money, allocate jobs and discuss the things brought to school by the children. These short sessions at the beginning of a school day make a familiar pattern to many teachers. In some schools, the children come in – even before the nine o'clock bell – in order to get on with the tasks they were working on the day before. Some of the children may come early to carry out routine chores such as cleaning out animal cages, arranging flowers and exhibitions and the like. This kind of homely, informal way to begin the school day is by no means confined to the new schools. Many teachers, whatever the age of their building, have tried to make coming to school a joy for the children. Indeed, for too many children, school is a happier place to be in than the home, and no school should be so rigid and tied down by unnecessary rules that coming to school should be yet another affliction in their lives. Entering school to carry out tasks in a civilized manner is a very different procedure from that which is sometimes still seen, when whistles blow and straight rows are formed in the playground, more in the manner of an 1870s military parade ground than an establishment concerned with the growth and education of young children.

Teachers may wish to collect their own children at the end of the day and spend perhaps as long as half an hour with them in order to consider together the day's work and discuss plans for the next day, or the development of a specific piece of work. Many teachers will take the opportunity to end the day by telling or reading stories or poems, or by enjoying some other happy occasion together. Hopefully, some children will go home to continue reading or to discuss their day's work with their parents. They may even enlist their parents' help, and return to school next day with more to contribute to the work of the group. A wise teacher will look for ways of obtaining parental involvement in the work of the school, for no child need believe that life inside school is completely divorced from his home life.

However, the times when a whole class meets its teacher may be kept to a minimum in schools where a timetable enables each teacher to have his own class at least once a day in a room at specified times. These will include the occasions when enclosable spaces are specifically timetabled for teachers and classes (see below). Often, the teacher will also take his own class for the usual periods of PE, movement, drama, music and other activities in the hall.

The concept of one child per desk is clearly irrelevant when children are in their 'own' home base for a few short times each day with their teacher. Indeed, the children will not even be able to have their own storage trays in their home bay or home room. They may need access to their own belongings at any time during the day, so the storage tray units must be available without a child having to enter a room and disturbing a teacher who may be in there with other children. For this reason, the children's storage trays (marked S S S in Figure 29) are placed *outside* rooms and bays so that they are available at any time. Reference books (B B B) are

F

81

also arranged around the perimeter of the open spaces for easy access during the day. Again they would be inaccessible to many children if they were contained within one room. The separate school library (Figure 26) could be used to house a fiction collection and special exhibits.

The same arguments may hold for the teachers' desks. If they were fixed in rooms, as in traditional classrooms, then the teachers could not easily interrupt colleagues in order to use their own desks. Perhaps the teachers' tables should also be placed in the large open area. Better still, some schools have now replaced teachers' desks with small wall-mounted bureaux with drop-down flaps. These are used by the teachers and hung wherever convenient. They have the considerable advantage of taking up no floor space. This is a valuable benefit especially if the reader compares this with the classrooms in Chapter 1 where the teacher's space may take up to a third of a classroom's floor space.

With morning class time and school assembly over, the children are free to move from their base and make use of all the facilities in the department. But this does not mean that children can have freedom to choose any activity they wish or to work in any space that is convenient to them. In fact, a timetable of teaching spaces is now needed so that every teacher and child knows what space is available. Indeed, the main idea behind the rest of this chapter is that conventional subject: timetables for junior school children may be replaced by timetables of spaces, with the teachers free to some extent to choose what they wish to teach, or – preferably – what they wish the children to learn, within the constraints determined by the allocation of spaces and the school's schemes of work.

Neither of the two units in the school taken as an example in this chapter could contain more than about ninety children (three class groups) in the large practical areas at any one time (Figure 30).

In actual practice, for some of the day, only about sixty children (two class groups) will be in the practical areas as one of the classes may be outside the unit, either in the hall or library or outside the building for games or swimming. In this way the best use of space is made in the school. Open plan schools have an advantage here over traditional buildings: when a class is using the hall in a traditional building, the classroom remains empty; in an open building, the removal of a class group from the teaching space gives more room for the other groups. This is an advantage which is too rarely recognized by critics of the new schools.

The allocation of rooms and bays will be made by the headteacher in consultation with the heads of each department and their assistants. There are many possibilities, and one of these is considered in detail. The system outlined here is based upon ideas used in some primary schools, and it depends upon the day being organized into four sessions, as follows:

9.30–10.30   1.30–2.30
10.45–11.45   2.45–3.45 (school finishes at 4.00)

82

Figure 30

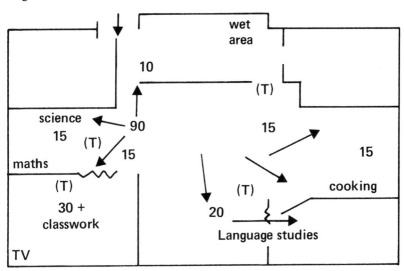

Like so much in a modern school, this fixed, apparently inflexible fragmentation of the day may be gradually modified as the school year continues. In due course, even the fixed playtimes may come to be abandoned as children and teachers see the advantages of taking a break at convenient times, and not when directed by the clock.

Each class group is timetabled to use the corner classroom (450 sq. ft.) with the television set for one hour per day. Here the teacher has her own class and there could be provision for each child to have his own chair and table-space. During this hour, rather more formal activities could take place, if desired. This is the teacher's opportunity to take a class lesson perhaps, with a blackboard at her side. There may be television programmes to watch and discuss. As the room is reasonably sound-proofed, the class could enjoy some music together. In this particular school there is no specific room for music, which is a considerable disadvantage. Every school needs a room where very quiet activities can take place, and noisy ones too. Most new schools have soundproofed 'quiet/noisy' rooms today, but the school in this instance is not so fortunate, and an enclosable room in each unit has to double as a 'quiet/noisy' room. The alternative is to have quiet and noisy activities in the school hall only.

The smaller room (350 sq. ft.) can also be used for class work, but it is perhaps too small for all thirty or more children to be seated at tables. Here, rather less formal work can go on, and children can spill into the carpeted bay. In both the room and the bay somewhat quieter activities, especially those involved with reading and writing, can continue, away from the movement further out in the practical areas. In order to have no more than about ninety children at any one time in the practical areas, it will be necessary to timetable the smaller room for class work for about one hour per day. For the remaining time, the room can be available as an extension of the practical areas, but with the reservation that quieter activities – especially language work – are to take place at that end of the unit.

Except for the periods in the classroom, the teachers are no longer teaching their own class of children for the whole day. Instead, they are spaced around the unit and are available to help any children. They *do* however, retain overall responsibility for their children's progress, and they keep the appropriate records. Headteachers would hope that their teachers have different strengths (e.g. art, mathematics, science, language, cooking etc), and they work mainly in the appropriate areas. However, they are *not* specialist teachers.

The organization described so far is based upon the timetabling of two enclosable rooms in each unit, and it is very simple to operate. It does allow for a sharing of the whole unit, and it permits many kinds of teaching. Class lessons, practical activities of both a noisy and quiet nature, individual work and research: all these have a place in the work of a school and are catered for by a simple timetable. The basic concept of one teacher – one class still operates for at least an hour a day, but for the remainder of the time there will be little opportunity for class teaching as in traditional schools to continue.

Figure 31 shows a typical timetable for a fourth year class of juniors, working in accordance with the organization described above. At the beginning of the year, each class of children is organized into five groups for much of the time. This is to enable them to cover different aspects of the curriculum – science, mathematics, environmental studies, art/craft etc. In this instance, there are two groups of children working at any one time on mathematics (so that each child will have a double allocation of time for this subject), science, art/craft and general studies (which covers all the many social and environmental studies, embracing far more than history and geography). These somewhat inflexible groupings can be gradually abandoned as each child develops his own skills and knowledge. Indeed, after a few weeks, the timetabled groupings of children (numbered 1 to 5 in the timetable shown) will become meaningless as children develop their own individual competences. But the timetable does provide a framework within which teachers and children are free to work. Also, a balance of work must be maintained, and the timetable does at least remind all involved of curricular aspects which must be tackled. There are, of course, large blocks of time (e.g. Monday afternoon, Wednesday morning, Friday afternoon) when the timetable is so flexible that children working at art, for example, need not finish by the clock. In fact, an

Figure 31

M	1 Science 2 G.S. 3 Art P 4 Maths 1 RECORDERS 5 Maths 2 L	GENERAL STUDIES TVR	1 M1 2 M2 3 Sc P 4 G.S. 5 A	GENERAL STUDIES P
T	1 M1 2 Sc 3 G.S. P 4 A 5 M2	LANGUAGE MATHS TVR	1 G.S. 2 A 3 M1 P 4 M2 5 Sc	GAMES
W	1 A 2 M1 3 M2 P 4 Sc 5 G.S.	1 M1 2 M2 3 Sc P 4 G.S. 5 A	GENERAL P.E. SR H	LANGUAGE MATHS GENERAL STUDIES TVR
T	1 M2 2 Sc 3 G.S. P 4 A 5 M1	GENERAL STUDIES CHOIR RECORDERS H or P (Flexible)	R.E. MATHS TVR	GENERAL P.E. L H
F	1 Sc 2 G.S. 3 A P 4 M1 5 M2	LANGUAGE MATHS TVR	1 G.S. 2 A 3 M1 P 4 M2 5 Sc	1 A 2 M1 3 M2 P 4 Sc 5 G.S.

P practical areas   H hall   TVR large, enclosable room with television set
L school library   SR small enclosable room   GS general studies

'integrated day' will gradually emerge, except for the periods when a class is timetabled into the hall or an enclosable room.

In Figure 32, a class of about thirty children are working according to the timetable shown previously. They are in their five groups, working alongside children in the groups from other classes. Thus about fifteen children (three groups from three classes) are working at each activity, perhaps somewhat fewer in the wet area. The teachers (T) are available to give guidance, although the children are working at assignments set by their own class teacher, after discussion at 'together-time' in the corner classroom.

Figure 32

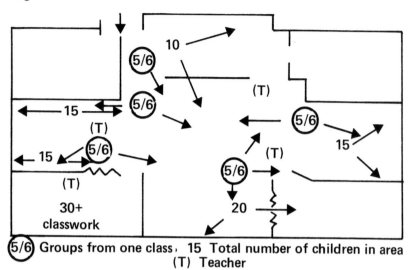

(5/6) Groups from one class 15 Total number of children in area
(T) Teacher

Children grouped for science and mathematics will be using books, work cards and apparatus in the appropriate bay, or in the adjacent open practical area. Children timetabled for general studies will use the large carpeted bay for quiet reading and writing studies, spilling into the small room. They may also work in the large practical area to prepare displays, make models etc. They have access to the wet area for paints, brushes and other equipment. This particular fourth year class does not have children scheduled to work in the cookery area, but a small group of children may use it if it is free. They may do this as part of an assignment in mathematics, science or general studies, or as an activity in its own right.

The timetable and the grouping of children may be seen as the framework within which teachers and children have a great deal of freedom to change activities or to work as individuals: no teacher would insist that a child should move away from a complex piece of work which is absorbing the child's interest simply because the timetable must be adhered to. Another value in this arrangement is that there is some control over who uses which space. It would be foolish to have one area crowded and other spaces empty, and some kind of outline organization is needed to make maximum use of space and facilities.

However, the main argument for an organization of grouping and space is the need to provide a balanced curriculum. It is important that all aspects of the child's development should be encouraged and stimulated: every school has a duty to see that no child's education is warped or out of balance. Decades ago, the child's aesthetic development was considered less important than intellectual development; today the modern schools provide for social and emotional as well as physical, aesthetic and intellectual growth. For this reason, the table below shows the balance of the curriculum as it works out in the organization already discussed.

The balance of the curriculum and the allocation of space

A fourth year class

Classrooms	*Language*	approximately 120 minutes (including some in general studies periods)
	Mathematics	approximately 120 minutes
	Social/environmental studies and general studies	approximately 90 minutes
Practical areas	30+ children in five groups	
	Each group: science studies, general studies, art/craft, maths 1, maths 2	2 x 60 minutes
Hall/outside	Drama	30 minutes
	PE	2 x 30 minutes
	Music	30–60 minutes
	Games/swimming	60 minutes
Library	Recorder group	30 minutes
	General	30 minutes

Now it may be argued that education cannot be measured in minutes, as shown above. Also, it may be legitimately argued that many activities cannot be categorized into any subject compartment: science, for example, has many affinities with differing aspects of knowledge and discovery which cannot be labelled in a school's timetable. Again, environmental studies may include much more than the traditional history and geography: for this reason, the label 'general studies' has been used above. In brief, the traditional subjects of a primary school do not give adequate scope for the many interests of juniors, and any categorization of subjects could endanger the necessary and desirable integration of subjects. Nevertheless, the table does show that a proper balance of different kinds of learning are taking place during any week, and that no child neglects, say, his mathematics or his physical education. It goes without saying that no child or teacher will work at subjects or activities to exact minutes, and the overall balance must be regarded liberally so that children's all-round development is continued over the whole school year. Possibly, in one week certain activities may be stressed, and the balance redressed later in the term. This kind of flexibility will require the teachers to work together in modifying the timetable as necessary. Much will depend upon the teachers' methods of keeping records of children's work and progress.

Obviously, the timetable for these children must relate to what the five teachers in the other unit are doing. The headteacher has to draw up a master timetable which will show the use being made of the hall and library by the teachers in both units (Figure 33).

Figure 33

Monday PERIODS					Tuesday PERIODS					Wednesday PERIODS				
CLASS	1	2	3	4	CLASS	1	2	3	4	CLASS	1	2	3	4
1	P	TVR	P	P	1	P/H	TVR	P	G	1	P	P	SR/H	TVR
2	TVR	P	P	G	2	TVR	P	P	H/P	2	P	TVR	P	P
3	P	P	TVR	P	3	P	P	TVR	P	3	H	P	P	G
4	P	H	P	TVR	4	H/P	P	G	P	4	TVR	P	P	P
5	H/L	P	SR	P	5	P	SR	P	TVR	5	P	SR	TVR	P

Thursday PERIODS					Friday PERIODS							
CLASS	1	2	3	4	CLASS	1	2	3	4	P	practical areas	
1	P	P/H	TVR	L/H	1	P	TVR	P	P	SR	small room	
2	TVR	P	P	P	2	TVR	P	P	P	H	hall	
3	P	H/P	P	TVR	3	P	P	TVR	P	L	library	
4	SR	TVR	P	P	4	H/P	SR	H/P	TVR	G	games	
5	P	P	SR	H/L	5	P/H	P	P/H	G	TVR	larger room with TV	

The master timetable is for the upper junior unit, and time is left for the hall to be available to the lower juniors. Even so, there need be no more than the three class groups (about ninety children) in the unit's practical areas at any one time. The hall must be used fully throughout the day. Tables for school dinners are not put out until 11.45 at the earliest, and they are away again by the time afternoon school commences.

Conclusion

The system outlined in this chapter is doubtless one of many possibilities. Every school is different and will be organized differently. There are however some general principles which, obvious though they may seem, nevertheless merit consideration. They are:

1   Maximum possible use of all available space. The hall, for example, should not stand empty, leaving children to be more crowded than necessary in the teaching areas.

2 By the same token, any enclosable rooms or quiet/noisy rooms should be used to the maximum.
3 The school should provide for a variety of teaching and learning experiences, e.g. whole school time (assembly), class time, occasions for more than one class to come together, time for small groups to work and for individuals to study.
4 Available space to be allocated and used fairly, but the teachers to have the freedom to adapt the space and the timetable as necessary, in order to integrate the work as much as possible.
5 A balanced curriculum to be maintained.

The above points require a master timetabling, mainly of space, when the headteacher and heads of units could plan together. The timetabling of learning activities and subjects is a separate but allied matter, and will require the attention of all a unit's teachers in consultation with the headteacher, who is ultimately responsible for the curriculum and syllabuses and schemes of work.

Such a system which aims to give the maximum flexibility and freedom within a minimum framework of planning requires an understanding of the responsibilities. Five teachers may work together well as a team, but it is a rare group of teachers which can be completely equal and democratic. The movements of staff from one school to another is common, and teaching teams are rapidly changed. Also, probationers and teachers new to open plan schools will need help in adjusting. In the interests of harmony and of giving leadership on matters of method and curriculum, the headteacher would have to appoint two strong unit heads. They should carry senior posts (and be paid accordingly), and they should be experienced and forward-looking teachers who are able to cooperate with the headteacher in running his school in a sound and enterprising fashion.

6 The teaching team

The teachers' role in open plan schools has been discussed in the various chapters concerned with the organization of teaching groups. Here we make some general comments, and consider the teaching team in a wider context. It is of limited value to think of the teaching force in a new school as a matter of class teachers with their groups of pupils, for many other people may be involved in the educative process within the school. What part does the headteacher play? To what extent may supernumerary teachers, ancillary helpers, students and parents be legitimately considered as part of the teaching team? It may well be that new relationships between children and adults will emerge in our schools, and here we consider some of the developments which have been taking place in recent years.

The headteacher
It is one of the ironies of our educational system that old schools have to be replaced irrespective of a headteacher's principles and beliefs. It frequently happens that a headteacher is opposed to the educational practices discussed in this book, yet he is required to lead the teaching team in an open plan situation. On the other hand, headteachers and staff may be practising many of the newer methods in their old schools with little hope of a new purpose-built school in which to continue their enterprising methods. It is hoped that some of the ideas expressed in this book will help the headteachers who are forced unwillingly into the new buildings. For many, a rethinking of their whole philosophy of teaching may be required. It is hoped that they will keep an open mind and encourage the innovations which younger members of staff might seek to try. They should also remember that a school is being built not only to suit their educational ideals, but also those of their successors, who may well be dedicated to the principles which originally led to the new kinds of school design.

Such is the freedom of the headteacher in our system that the success of any individual school will ultimately depend, in large measure, on him. Fortunately, in all but the largest primary schools, the headteacher can continue to regard himself primarily as a teacher of children, and not solely as an administrator. Many headteachers – even of very large schools – make the time to teach regularly and to keep in touch with the day-to-day work of their staff. The headteacher leads his staff by the example he sets. Over and above this he has the duty of planning and developing policy. The school atmosphere, its ideals, successes and standards will depend upon him. He will have to make the final decision about introducing innovations or discarding past practices.

But the headteacher's policies can be implemented in practice only in so far as he carries the staff with him, and organizes effectively the structure of the teaching situations in the available spaces. The organization of the school will reflect the headteacher's ideals, but there are hard decisions to make which he has to match to these. Child development theory should form the basis of all our work in primary schools, but the head must also make firm decisions of management and organization which allow for a framework within which the theories can be put into practice. Thus, senior appointments have to be made, but these decisions have to be taken in a hardheaded professional manner. Teachers should not always be automatically promoted because they have served for a long time on the staff. Deputies, heads of departments and team leaders can often be paid above the basic scales in the larger schools, and these appointments should be made for the good of the whole school and not as a reward for long service. Promotion should be linked to extra responsibility.

The one chore of primary school organization that need no longer take up hours of a headteacher's time is that concerned with the structuring of a detailed timetable. Most modern primary schools work in large blocks of time – quarter, half or whole days – with the headteacher being required only to specify the spaces that teachers have to share (e.g. hall for PE, quiet/noisy room). Most heads have abandoned the timetable which breaks up the day into half-hours of different subjects. This does not mean that the headteacher abandons his overall view of the activities which teachers and children pursue. The planning of syllabuses or schemes of work is a vital part of the head's work.

The headteacher's duties are many and varied. Internally he has of course the fundamental responsibility for the welfare and education of every child. But in order to undertake this central duty he has to be in touch with many people outside the school.

The role of the headteacher
Internal
Working with children
Meeting children's parents
Arranging pre-reception visits for parents and children
Discussing with teachers how parents might be involved in the life of the school, and initiating the involvement
Advising parents with problems

Leading the teaching team
Organizing the further professional education of the teaching team
Helping and guiding probationer teachers
Organizing and allocating teaching spaces and time
Classifying records of children's progress and difficulties
Ordering and allocating equipment and supplies, in consultation with teachers
Discussing and determining the curriculum priorities
Evolving schemes of work
Leading the ancillary team (clerical, caretaking, kitchen, crossing-patrol staff)
Involving students in the work of the school
Inspiring a high sense of standards among pupils and teachers

External
Meeting children's parents
Involving the school in the life of the community
Representing the school at community and LEA functions
Meeting and planning with school managers
Working in cooperation with education officers
Working with educational psychologists, advisers and inspectors
Liaising with colleagues in secondary and other primary schools
Working with medical and welfare services
Helping in the in-service education of teachers at teachers' centres
Helping in the initial education of teachers by liaising with a college of education
Liaising with parks and swimming baths supervisors

In what ways are these duties different for the head of an open plan school as opposed to a school of conventional design?

The headteacher's role is the same in any primary school, but in an open plan situation his mode of operating is different. Inevitably team work has to replace teaching in isolated boxes, and the headteacher of necessity becomes more involved in the open situation, functioning as a 'leader' rather than as a possibly remote authoritarian figure. He influences the whole school by establishing good personal relationships with members of staff and by initiating cooperative approaches. He will need to consult his teachers more often and involve them in evaluating the content of what is being learned and taught, and he will lead constant reappraisal of the methods, organization and assessment of children's progress. In short, headteachers in open plan schools are responsible for providing in-service education for the teachers. The termly staff meeting is hardly sufficient for this. Many schools hold regular lunch-time or after school 'workshops' of the staff so that problems and policies can be discussed informally. Occasionally the staff meet during a school closure to hammer out difficulties together. Most headteachers today require all their staff to come into school before the start of a new academic year so that children and teachers do not come fresh into the situation on the first day of term. Often teachers will stay after school to debate a matter, or to become involved in a particular item of curriculum development, for example, by watching an educational programme on TV (teachers' programmes are frequently screened at 4.15 pm so that a whole staff may view then and discuss the implications before going home at about 5.0 pm).A head-teacher with strong views on primary education will want to influence others in the profession, and headteachers frequently run local courses in cooperation with advisers and wardens of teachers' centres.

Some headteachers reading these paragraphs will comment that their job is so demanding that there is little time to work with children. But, such is the variety of human nature, that one can visit two schools of similar size and with comparable difficulties, and find one headteacher coping just about adequately, while the other leads dynamically and affects beneficially the whole lives of the teachers, the children and their parents. The character, success and reputation of a school reflects the quality of the headteacher's contribution, and it can truly be said of primary schools that 'where there's a will, there's a way'.

Assistant teachers

The size of the team
Open plan schools are built to many different designs, and the layout will determine the number of teaching groups which will share a space. Sometimes large teams of six or more teachers will work together (Chapter 5), but more usually the team will consist of either two, three or four teachers. The larger the team the more complex will the organization need to be, but there are few new schools which are so large and open that more than six or seven teachers have to work together sharing the spaces and resources. In schools where large teams work together (as described in Chapter 5) it could be argued that the larger the teaching team the more expertise there will be available for the benefit of the children. Six teachers will mean at least six different teaching strengths to be immediately on call within the team. Some educationists would claim that large groups of teachers working in a large shared space will soon break down into smaller teams. Certainly it is often observed that two or three teachers out of the half-dozen or more will combine their efforts, and sub-groups will naturally occur.

What then is the best size of the teaching team? If the primary school curriculum is broken down into its main components, it may well be that this will give a guide. Language, mathematics and the creative arts are three clear aspects of the curriculum, although they can all overlap and integrate with each other. Certainly a team of two teachers can share the basic work in language and mathematics and advise each other from their own particular strength. A third teacher may become the arts/crafts leader in the team. But a two or three teacher team may also have to offer music, PE, environmental studies, French and science to the children. Either each member of the team must be responsible for at least two aspects of the curriculum, or each one should offer general subjects plus one or more special subjects. Most headteachers will wish to continue the primary school tradition of the teacher as a general practitioner, but with each one advising colleagues on a certain aspect of the curriculum. It seems that the curriculum itself gives no exact indication of the best size of team in a primary school (though it may well do so in a secondary school where teachers' specialisms are more apparent), but there seems to be a growing belief in schools that three or four teachers in a team will cover the curriculum reasonably well, without a loss of flexibility. In the long run the best size of team is the one that will lead to harmony and willing cooperation, and this indicates that a team of two, three or four teachers will be more likely to produce this than a larger one which could well include a clash of personalities or a teacher opposed to the whole system.

The numbers of pupils involved is also a relevant factor. With an average pupil:teacher ratio of about 35:1 a four teacher unit contains 140 children, and this may be as large a number of children that any teacher would wish to see in any one shared space. For many teachers, smaller units of two or three teaching groups (70 or 105 children respectively) would be more satisfactory, and smaller groups based on a ratio of 30:1 (giving 60 or 90 children) would be ideal.

Each member of the team will contribute to the general work of the unit, and there will have to be continuous discussion and interchange of views. In most situations, one of the teachers will have to be clearly designated as team leader, with a responsibility to the headteacher for the work of the team. Her role will be similar to that of a headteacher in a small village school, except that she must establish links with other teams in the school. Her team will almost certainly contain one teacher who is specially trained, or very interested, in language development and the teaching of reading. This teacher will not assume the role of a specialist teacher: indeed, the task of coping with the reading progress of a hundred or more children would be a most tedious one. Instead she would act as the language 'consultant' or 'adviser' in the team and would have responsibility for furthering the work of all the teachers and children in this area of the curriculum. This will include giving advice to colleagues on methods to use and equipment to be obtained. She will also have responsibility for the language resource material in the unit or department and the organization of the central language resource area. She will consult with the team leader and headteacher on books and equipment to be ordered and the spending of the money available. She will attend courses on language and reading and pass on her expertise to colleagues through the headteacher's in-service organization within the school. The rest of her day-to-day work will be as a general class teacher with her own teaching group. The teaching team may well also contain the mathematics consultant/adviser, and possibly one for creative arts. Other subjects in a three teacher unit will be covered by the teacher as in a normal class-teacher situation, sometimes with advice from a teacher in another team with greater knowledge of some subjects.

This breakdown of a team, with its specialists — consultants — advisers, will work in most situations. But an extension of this concept towards the specialist subject teachers of the secondary school is not appropriate at the primary level.

Many advantages are claimed for the cooperative system of teaching over the conventional class-teacher organization in separate classrooms. Each teacher's specific talents are available for all the children taught by the team: new teachers, including probationers, are more easily absorbed and find more security in an ongoing teaching situation where they can develop professional skills alongside the established teachers. A weak teacher, too, is helped by the team situation, and staff absences can be more easily covered because the existing staff know the children and can help a supply teacher to take over more easily. Again, the school's money will go further when a team will need only one language or mathematics resource centre as against the need for one per classroom in a conventional school. A strong argument too is that the absence of one teaching group (perhaps in the hall for PE) means more spaces for all the other children, whereas a normal classroom will remain empty as wasted teaching space when its children are out of the room.

But there can be disadvantages working against cooperative teaching unless the team leader and headteacher take particular care. A school may contain an uncooperative teacher, and nobody can *make* a person cooperate if he does not wish to do so. Sometimes good teachers can carry weaker colleagues who cannot, or will not, pull their weight. Also materials can be wasted unless care is taken. However, the main concern of teachers who are suspicious of the new methods is the possibility of children wasting their time or, perhaps through timidity, not fulfilling their potential. This problem may be coupled to the parent's bewilderment, for all teachers know of the mother who says, 'but I do want Johnny to go into Miss Smith's class'.

These last two points are the most challenging to teachers: parents must be consulted and reassured (Chapters 3 and 9) and careful tabs must be kept on children's work and progress.

Keeping records
Record keeping takes thought, time, and careful organization. It can also be burdensome. Therefore a teaching team should try to strike a balance: on the one hand, records should not be so detailed as to be irksome to compile, and they should not contain material which is of little positive value; on the other hand, records should be full enough to keep account of what really needs to be known about each child.

Most primary schools wish to compile their own internal records on each child, and there are many ways of doing this. To some extent children keep their own records (e.g. in working through a structured reading programme), but teachers still need to discuss the activities and examine the work produced, in order to assess each child's progress. Actual pieces of work produced by each child and kept in a personal folder are probably the best record of the child's academic progress, while a 'profile' of the child will cover other areas of development and give relevant background information. For the development of language skills and mastery of reading, teachers keep records on what the child has read, the dates when books in a reading scheme were completed and a score sheet of phonics, digraphs etc which are crossed out as the child masters them. The results of standardized tests plot a child's progress over a longer period and help to identify problems: added notes on a child's special difficulties can also be valuable. For progress in writing, it is becoming common for schools to file away pieces of the child's written work taken at random at intervals through the infant and junior years.

Many schools keep simple checklists covering a child's understanding of mathematical concepts. It is difficult to compile checklists for most of the other aspects of the curriculum, but there should be some means of noting the work produced by the children in such subjects as environmental studies or religious education.

For infant teachers especially, it is thought by many to be good practice for general aspects of child development to be noted: his physical, social, emotional and intellectual development could be noted, perhaps by the teacher jotting down a continuous log of his observations on the child's powers of concentration, his attitudes to learning, his social adjustment and emotional stability. In addition, important happenings in a child's life may be noted, especially if they affect his development (e.g. illness, death of a relative or other cause of emotional stress).

It is customary for teachers to keep a record of work attempted by the children, and some headteachers ask for a weekly forecast and/or a diary. These will be of little value if they merely list the activities provided. However, the anecdotal-type diary which is based on the teacher's observation and which indicates the level of involvement and degree of understanding of individual children when engaged on different activities is useful both to the class teacher and to the head. It is helpful to the class teacher in that it clarifies her thinking and helps her to plan ahead, and it gives the sort of assessment of teaching situations and children's progress which the headteacher requires.

However, the basic duty of providing for continuity and progression of experiences has to be attempted and should be recorded. Somehow a school must avoid the woolly 'hit or miss' coverage of themes and topics which is too often seen in some primary schools. A balance must be achieved between too much and too little recording, and the school staff, together with the head, need to decide what, how and when to record within the school. Records which are passed on to other schools should also be agreed, either between the schools concerned, or by the authority for all schools. Each receiving secondary school will have its own priorities, depending on whether the intake is to be organized in mixed-ability classes or banded, setted or streamed. It is highly desirable for junior and secondary schools to get together in order to discuss the recording system for a catchment area, and this is a valuable task for teachers' centres to undertake.

The supernumerary teacher

Some local authorities have been trying to staff primary schools more generously in recent years, and it is not uncommon for a large primary school to have a full-time or part-time member of staff who does not normally have a post as a class teacher. In conventional schools, such a 'floating' teacher would relieve class teachers, take small groups of children for remedial work or teach classes for specialist work (e.g. music, French, PE). In an open plan situation, the extra teacher may well join a team — for example, 140 children would be taught by five instead of four teachers, and the extra teacher would work as a normal member of the team with the children in their mixed-ability groups. In the larger schools, the supernumerary may spend days or half-days with different teams or departments. In some schools, the headteacher may decide to employ the extra teacher for work with slow learners or with children of normal ability who need remedial help (see Chapters 3 and 4).

Most schools do have problems with slow learners and children needing remedial teaching, and it is usually thought necessary to give these pupils some special help. In an infant school or department the headteacher frequently takes small groups of children, or individuals, for special coaching, usually for reading. It is rare and undesirable to find a special class for slow learners in an infant school, even in a very large one, and any supernumerary would probably work alongside the rest of the teaching team.

In the larger junior schools and departments, there may be a strong case for employing the supernumerary teacher as the person responsible for helping the slower learners and remedial children, either in withdrawal groups or in a permanent special class. Such a class would rarely hold more than about twenty children, and the teacher would preferably have had some special training in helping these children. Thus the children would establish a permanent relationship with one teacher and they would work to a special programme and curriculum devised in the light of the teacher's extra training and understanding. There are disadvantages in having a special slow learners' class — there is always the possibility of a stigma becoming attached to the class, and the selection of the children may become self-validating, i.e. there may be a lower sense of achievement in the class so the children do not reach a true level of aspiration. Again, the organization of a special class may not fit easily into the organization of an open plan school, for such a class may require one of the few enclosable spaces throughout the day, thus depriving all the other children of access to a quiet/noisy room. For these and other reasons, depending on the circumstances in the school (such as the availability of a quiet place for a small group), the headteacher may prefer a trained supernumerary to take special groups according to a withdrawal system. Such a system will avoid the stigma which may become attached to children in a permanent special class, but a disadvantage may be that a child is withdrawn for special help with, say, reading, when the necessary techniques for learning reading skills would be better acquired in a situation where reading is not divorced from other aspects of development and education. It is important too that a supernumerary remedial teacher with withdrawal groups should establish regular contacts with the members of the teaching teams, and especially with the home-base teachers of every child in the withdrawal group, so that there can be a regular exchange of views. Too often one sees remedial teachers working quite independently of what the class or home-base teacher is doing with the same children for the rest of the day.

Obviously, the use made of a supernumerary teacher for remedial work will depend a great deal on the circumstances in which the school finds itself. In some cases the extra teacher would be better employed in helping colleagues in a team situation, or in releasing a class teacher who has continuous contact with the children and who can then find the time to provide some special educational treatment to children who need it. In the larger schools, the deputy head may be free of permanent teaching commitments and, with the headteacher, is free instead to work in the different teams or to take special groups.

It is not unknown for the headteacher in a conventional school to refuse the appointment of a supernumerary teacher. This happens because there is a teacher for every classroom leaving no room available where the extra teacher could work. In open plan schools this, at least, would be no problem, and most headteachers would find very good use for the extra teacher.

Cooperative teaching can be more challenging and interesting than teaching one's own class in a room throughout the school year. It can be refreshing for a teacher to have other adults near at hand: indeed it is surely a more natural situation for an adult to work alongside mature colleagues than to be isolated with children for most of the day. The experience can be good for both teachers and children, as they feed each other with ideas and learn that cooperation is more important for the education of human beings than competition. The situation can be even richer if the people involved are not always either teachers or pupils: other adults have a place in school too.

Ancillary assistants

Other adults on the permanent staff of schools include caretakers, school meal helpers, kitchen staffs and secretaries. These of course do not have any teaching functions in the schools. However, they are a part of the learning situation because they establish relationships with each other and with the children. Harmonious and cooperative social relationships will be of value to the children, and the example put before them will influence their own attitudes and values. Occasionally a headteacher may enlist the help of the ancillary staff in the work with children: the caretaker may show a group of boys how the plumbing works, the dinner-helper talks to children at lunchtime, making the occasion a social and educational one. But these of course are peripheral. In recent years a step has been made by many authorities to employ second-tier workers who have a specific task to help the teachers. These are the welfare or ancillary assistants who help to care for some of the needs of the children in the learning situation. They are coming to be greatly valued, for teachers find that they can be relieved to some extent of many of the chores which waste their time and contribute little to the teaching.

Many authorities employ trained nursery nurses as ancillary workers in infant schools. These girls and women, whose training entails knowledge of child development and the value of play, make a most welcome contribution to the learning situation. Working under the teacher's direction and guidance they can become involved in a number of activities, supervising, helping and talking to the children. They read or tell stories to the children and help them mount work and assemble displays. They supervise the children's hand-washing and help with changing of clothes. They make apparatus under the teacher's direction, laminate work cards, and undertake a hundred other useful tasks, and thus release the teacher for more important teaching duties.

It is becoming widely recognized that the trained welfare ancillary is a great asset in the open plan situation where she works as a member of the team. Each unit ought to have at least one such trained ancillary. Many teachers' centres now run short courses for untrained assistants, helping them to grasp the educational implications of their work and showing them how they can help the teachers. Some of the duties, especially in junior schools, will require training, for ancillaries frequently help with audio-visual aids, taping radio lessons or setting up equipment.

Students

For many years now colleges have realized that there should not be a dichotomy between the students' studies in the college and his teaching on school practice. Some colleges do provide opportunities for students to learn in many different ways other than in the lecture situation. Unfortunately, school practice is still too often divorced from the rest of the students' course. In some cases work in schools becomes a series of interruptions in the three-or four-year courses, whereas what is needed is to bring the theory and practice of education together so that school practice becomes an integral part of a college course. There have been many experiments to make a students' school experience a central part of his training for the profession.

Sometimes full-time school practice is part of an ongoing process. Each student is attached to a school for a year, and he visits regularly before and after the short full-time practice period. Few colleges now expect students to visit a school only once or twice before the block practice begins. A regular contact with a school – perhaps as much as one day per week in the school for a year – has the advantage that the student can see children develop over a lengthy period, and he can also undertake long-term studies of children.

Another method of preparing students for open plan schools is to send students to the schools on a long-term basis and not only for a short four- or five-week spell. In one new school, each class teacher has one, and sometimes two, students with her throughout the whole school year. The students change every few weeks (although they all keep in contact with the school for their follow-up studies), and they play a regular, accepted part in school life, instead of being the occasional additions to the staff for a few weeks every year. In this way, large numbers of students are given the opportunity to become involved in the work of an open plan school, and they also provide some help for the teacher who often can make good use of an extra pair of hands during the school day.

This kind of student experience is very different from traditional school practice, when a student learns to replace the teacher in a classroom situation. Instead, the student works and learns alongisde the teacher, helping groups of children and perhaps taking larger groups of children for story work, music and the like. An important part of his work is his growing understanding of children and the notes on this that he matches to his theory courses. It is of vital importance that all newly-trained primary school teachers should have some understanding of new methods and open plan schools. How is this to be achieved when the student finds himself in a traditionally-built school? A method of helping students in conventional classroom situations is to encourage them to organize the room, or part of it, along the lines discussed in Chapter 1. Thus, in a junior classroom, the student could innovate after a while by organizing a science table or a library corner, for example. He would need to do this with the least possible disturbance to the routine of the school or class, and then to develop his innovations slowly. For a final school practice many class teachers will allow a student to change the room into an open plan situation for the last two or three weeks of the practice. Any external examiner, so much dreaded by students, will understand the compromises that have to be made in schools if students are going to be trained for modern teaching.

The role of a student in an open plan school will ultimately be the same as that of a student in a conventional situation. That is, he will take over the duties of a general-purpose class teacher for a few weeks. But in preparation for this the student will be considered as a kind of apprentice (on the long-term basis described above) helping the teacher where he çan and gradually gaining experience with individual children and with groups.

Given a flexible college organization, students could be a regular part of the teaching team in an infant or junior school, just as NNEB students are in our nursery schools.

Parents

In Chapter 3 there is some indication of how teachers can make contact with parents in order to break down the barriers which may exist between home and school. Some teachers go further and invite parents to participate in the work with the children inside the school. In a sense parents can become a part of the school's teaching team, although their work in the teaching situation is not of a professional nature. A list of parents' activities which would complement those of teachers will give some of the possibilities:

assisting with the preparation of craft materials
making and mending apparatus and toys
making costumes for plays
helping in the library
laundering the football team's shirts and pants
tidying bookshelves and tables
playing the piano as an accompanist
laminating work cards
arranging flowers
hearing groups of able children read (i.e. as a listener – not a teacher)
helping with the distribution of milk (infants)
fathers doing 'odd jobs' – making display stands, goalposts, repairing
    school furniture
helping at school functions – sports days, concerts etc
helping teachers on out-of-school visits and excursions
helping the children to prepare and bake cakes
helping to decorate part of the school for Christmas festivities

Many teachers will wonder about the wisdom of involving parents in the school's teaching situation. Indeed, some teachers have noted that parents in their enthusiasm to help will do far too much for the children, so that educational opportunities are missed. Nevertheless, in many schools parents are welcomed, if only to provide extra pairs of hands as a help to teachers. Headteachers will know that general invitations to all parents could cause problems, but on the other hand he cannot reasonably organize a selection procedure. This is an instance where the headteacher's judgement and local knowledge will come into play. A tactful headteacher will devise different levels of involvement for different parents. Some who have little to offer in the teaching situation could be usefully employed elsewhere in the school. He might also profitably give parents who are to be involved in the teaching situation some instruction about their role before introducing them into the team.

Other adults and visitors

Mention has been made of the school's adult workers other than the teachers. Occasionally adults come in from outside to work with the children. Policemen instruct on road safety, and firemen visit and talk with the children. Enterprising teachers leading the children in an exciting project may bring in people to talk informally to groups of children: in one school the milkman, the foreman of the new school's building site, the architect of the new school, a veterinary surgeon, the borough librarian and the school doctor – all these came into the school at one time or another during the year to talk to groups of children. Clearly, these visits helped the children to learn about their community and established a bridge between the school and the outside world.

Many sixth formers and other secondary school children are considering careers which will involve them with children, and these teenagers are sometimes to be seen in primary schools. In one school A level candidates from a girls' grammar school spent afternoons in an infant school by rota: they were girls who were applying for college of education places or for other work with children. There has been a growing trend for secondary school youngsters to visit primary schools as part of some communtiy course for CSE or non-examination work. This situation will have to be carefully watched, for young children can feel overwhelmed and become adversely affected by too much attention. Secondary school children should only visit primary schools in ones and twos, and if the intention is that they should be helpful, then they must be carefully briefed before visiting the school. In such circumstances they can prove useful and therefore they are welcome in the primary school.

Conclusion

This chapter has tried to show how adults of different skills and experience can work together in a team which helps children to learn. Trained teachers lead the team, and other adults are involved in different ways. It may well be that all primary schools are moving to a position similar to that existing in nursery schools, where qualified teachers are supported by a second tier of adults (nursery nurses). This need not lead to a dilution of the teaching profession: in nursery schools the ratio of teachers to pupils is not affected because nursery nurses are at hand to help the teachers. In open plan infant and junior schools parents, students, ancillaries and others may be available to support the teachers. But this does not mean that there will be fewer teachers for the children. The Plowden Report stated that 'a class teacher cannot satisfactorily work with more than thirty to thirty-five children', and this holds good no matter how many second-tier adults are involved in the work of the teaching team.

7 The learning environment

Several times already reference has been made to the learning environment. It has been said for instance that children must be welcomed into a safe, secure situation where there are all sorts of interesting and intriguing things which will encourage them to talk and think and do. It has also been stated that all children should be acquiring new knowledge based on previous experience. It is recognized that all children are different because of their background, heredity and experience, and that all children pass through the same stages of development but at different ages. Children experience spurts and plateaux in development and may exhibit various learning characteristics, in that one child may learn more readily through visual experience and another through hearing or touch.

Learning begins for the very young child through play and sensory experience. At first he is concerned with objects and people in isolation and later begins to see relationships between them. He expresses the impressions he has gained, through language acquired from the people round about him.

The ideal learning environment, therefore, is one in which the differences between individuals are recognized and met by a variety of provisions, including both the familiar and the new, and which allows each child to take from it what he needs at any given time. It allows the child to understand relationships and to come to terms with the world in which he lives. It gives the child opportunity to build up concepts, not by being told things in the abstract, but by being able to look and listen, to handle and do things for himself, and so build up composite ideas about his environment. The emphasis at all times is on understanding: understanding comes from experience and needs time to grow.

The young child in school does not separate his learning into subject areas – he simply learns – and it is impossible to consider any one aspect of education in isolation. Hence the provision of an integrated approach such as that described in Chapters 2 and 4, in which children may be observed working singly or in small groups, handling concrete apparatus and equipment, through which they acquire understanding.

The modern infant learning environment provides a mixture of the familiar and the new. Children settle more easily and quickly in surroundings where they encounter familiar things. All children have a common experience of 'home' with its furnishings and various members of the family, although it is recognized (see Chapter 9) that the homes vary considerably in quality. It is comforting to small children to find in the home-play area, furniture and fitments similar to those at home, albeit somewhat smaller. Here they can re-create the situations they know best and with the aid of the dressing-up box can take on the roles of absent adults. In these familiar secure surroundings they acquire confidence to try out other new experiences which are also available.

Many small children will also have had experience at home of various toys, bricks and puzzles. They may have had access to books, to painting, crayonning and paper and pencils. Some lucky children will have heard stories, rhymes and songs told or sung by their mothers and all children are likely to have experience of radio and television.

In the home children are often provided with facilities but are then left to their own devices. Only the lucky few will have had the delight of sharing their experiences with their parents. Where there is no adult participation the standard of play may not have progressed very far, and where there is no adult intervention, language development is also likely to be retarded. Some parents, for example, use the television set as a child-minder, or mechanical educator. They sit their children in front of the set, very often irrespective of the material being shown, and assume that the children will learn from it. These parents quite overlook the fact that this is only one-way communication. The set certainly furnishes information, but the child cannot ask it questions or receive answers, so that much of the information is misunderstood, and instead of learning, complete incomprehension ensues. Television programmes need to be shared with an adult for the child to get the best from them.

The school uses the familiar experiences of the child and builds on to them: situations are similar but the provision is much more varied. Instead of the pale water-colours and inadequate brushes usually provided at home, the child finds large brushes and bold colours. He is able to experiment with finger paints, to handle clay and dough, and to make things from scrap materials using paste and scissors or from wood using hammers, saws and glue. There are musical instruments to play and music to move to, alone or in company with others. Instead of a few books the school provides hundreds for the child to look at, read and enjoy.

Often when the child first comes to school the parent proudly announces 'he can count'. Once in school these words chanted to please parents, begin to take on meaning and acquire significance as the child collects objects into groups, recognizes similarities and differences and begins to classify them under the guidance of the teacher. The child begins to see for instance that five remains the same unless something is added to it or taken from it. He learns that it can be made up in a variety of ways from a variety of objects and that five lots of five make something else again.

Teachers then provide situations familiar to the child and help him to make sense of them. They supply materials and pose problems, and then watch what the child does, and finally discuss with him what he has done. The teacher recognizes that there must be adult intervention if a child's learning is to develop. Intervention must, however, be very sensitive. Children who are engrossed in their own patterns of learning through play and who are not yet ready to move on to a new step or a new activity, may resent what to them is simply interruption or interference. They indicate when this is the case, by continuing in their own way and ignoring the well-meant but untimely suggestions of the teacher. Teachers need to be able to follow the child's line of thought in order to be able to pose the right question at the right time. They should recognize that children do not always think in the way expected of them and that often the child's own line of thought is more appropriate for true understanding to develop and is, therefore, more productive.

It is well known that doing things and talking about what we are doing often results in deeper understanding. Only by observing what each child is doing and talking to him about what he has done can the teacher hope to measure the child's understanding — or lack of it. For example a child of ten who was very interested in geology had collected some rocks and was writing about them. He had weighed them and had recorded that one of the rocks was 'about three stone'. When asked if he could be more accurate he said that he could not as when he had weighed the rock at home on the bathroom scales it had weighed just over three stone and on the scales at school it had been just under three stone. The teacher asked him what conclusion he had drawn from this, thinking that the boy would say the scales were inaccurate. Instead the boy explained that the school scales were too small to weigh the rock accurately. Intrigued, the teacher asked him to show her what he meant. He fetched the scales which were small and the rock overlapped the weighing surface considerably. The boy indicated the areas of rock overhanging the edge of the scales and said 'you see it isn't weighing those bits so I have to guess'. This boy had moved house several times in his school life and somewhere in moving had missed some basic experience in weighing. The teacher was enabled by this conversation to discover this lack of experience and proceeded to devise situations which would help the boy fill in the gaps in his knowledge. The learning environment must be one where personal relationships are such that a free and frank exchange is possible between children and teacher, and that provided in the open plan school gives the child a better range of provision, a greater choice of activity and more room in which to work. An even greater advantage is the availability of a number of interested adults, be they teachers or other members of the team. In the classroom situation children have usually only one teacher to whom to refer. In the open plan unit the child has access to several teachers, a welfare ancillary, and from time to time students, visitors, and voluntary helpers as well. He has, therefore, several interested adults who between them possess different skills and interests to whom he can turn for help and advice. The availability of extra pairs of hands made possible in the open plan unit, releases the teachers to observe and talk to the children, to assess their understanding and to guide them on to further learning.

Sharing facilities and space can present problems for the teachers. Personal relationships between members of the team in an open plan unit are tremendously important and the headteacher must consider this point carefully when asking members of staff to work together. Children are very perceptive and soon recognize when adults are at loggerheads. It is wise, therefore, to prepare for cooperative teaching and reach agreement about such matters as practice and standards. Where there is such agreement relationships remain happy.

Display
Display is one area of the learning environment which is not valued sufficiently by some teachers. Often displays are set up for aesthetic appreciation only. This is, of course, important and display should always be of a high standard. Work should be well mounted, and thought be given to design and placement. Captions should be well written, legible and of uniform size, and the whole should be eye-catching and aesthetically pleasing. Some walls are literally covered from top to bottom with unrelated pieces of work and without any concern for the overall appearance. It is difficult to pick out anything of real interest and even the children have problems in identifying their own pieces of work. Such display is useless. Teachers who value display properly use it not only for its intrinsic aesthetic interest but also as a teaching tool.

Displays are often used to introduce children to new ideas and few primary schools are without a display of some kind. Sometimes these are based on a particular theme and may be set up in an entrance hall or some central area. The main purpose is to arouse interest and to stimulate children to explore the possibilities of items displayed in a variety of ways — a starting point for individual research or group activities.

Most infant classrooms have their own displays often based on a colour as quite a number of young children arrive at school unsure of colours. These usually consist of a drape (or drapes) tastefully arranged, on a variety of levels, as a background to a number of interesting articles on the particular colour involved. The display can then be used as a basis for talk between teacher and children, either as individuals, in small groups or as a class. There is a great number of shades within any particular colour and, with the teacher's encouragement, children begin to discriminate between light and dark, bright and dull, strong and weak, vivid and muted shades whilst realizing that all these belong to the same colour. The children learn new words and the meanings of words. Gradually too they realize that different surfaces and textures give rise to different shades of the same colour. They can pick things up and handle them, and under the teacher's guidance can consider where else they have seen articles of that particular colour or shade, either elsewhere in the building, or outside, so relating the colours to other situations and making use of memory.

Displays can be many and varied. They can be based on texture, shape, size, sound, taste and smell, involving all areas of sensory discrimination. Collections of glass, china, metal objects, or articles of historical, geographical or scientific interest can all be exploited in a similar fashion, giving children actual experience with real objects and providing opportunities to classify, discriminate and make choices. Displays of the children's own work can in turn give rise to discussion and may lead on to further learning. Children can be critical from an early age, not only of other people's work, but also of their own. The teacher will, of course, ensure that such criticism is friendly and constructive so that children are encouraged to improve on previous efforts.

Sometimes a single object exhibited in a prominent position with a caption such as 'What do you think this is?' can lead to imaginative talk and writing. The teacher's questions and comments need to be carefully chosen to stimulate the child to think and become communicative. The right question will provoke the child to speculate about the object, or to recall where he has seen something similar or to project his thoughts into the past or future or even into the realms of fantasy.

What has been said about display is relevant to any kind of school and it has been stated that the open plan unit can present problems with regard to display. It also has advantages. The open plan unit enables display to be used to the full. However good the display in the individual classroom it is usually only seen by, and at the disposal of, the children based in that classroom. In the open plan situation it is available to a greater number of children. It can also be used in a greater variety of ways. Teachers in a shared area are able to comment on each other's display and suggest additional ways in which it could be used. Teachers in such situations also learn from one another's display techniques, which results in a raising of standards. A good general standard of display and presentation serves as an example to the children whose work, in turn, improves.

As soon as children lose interest in a particular display it should be dismantled, and a new one set up. The length of interest varies and some displays give rise to more work than others. In the open plan situation it is important that all staff should agree when a display is no longer required, even if it was originally assembled by one member of staff for her own group of children: others may still wish to use it.

Another advantage provided by the open plan unit is that a display of one group of children's work can be used to stimulate another group to work at a different level. For example, a class of infants who had made a collection of Autumn leaves, had sorted them into sets. These had been arranged on a background and exhibited on a wall in the unit, part of which was also used by junior children. Later that day a card appeared below the display. This had been prepared by one of the junior teachers, and posed various questions about the sets to be answered by the juniors.

107

Work shared in such a way adds to the feeling of unity and common purpose within the school and indicates that the same material can be used to advantage in different ways at different levels.

Standards

Many people fear that open plan schools may result in a lowering of standards generally. It seems as though they correlate removal of interior walls with removal of limits; that children please themselves whether they work or not, and that movement and noise is unrestrained. It is hoped that previous chapters will have done something to dispel these notions.

The Plowden Report indicated that schools differ in quality, not only with regard to buildings but also in what goes on inside them. Open plan schools also fall into different categories: some are good, others average and a few indifferent. In the well-run, efficient open plan schools standards are usually high.

Socially the open plan school might seem to present a problem in that a far greater number of individuals are in contact with one another. In fact this appears to be beneficial: because greater numbers are involved conscious effort is made to make the situation acceptable. Architects, recognizing that greater numbers could produce greater noise, treat the building acoustically so that noise is deadened. Teachers agree on common standards, accept a certain level of noise in a working situation and children recognize the limits set. Then too they are encouraged from the outset to consider other people. If children make too much noise they are quietly reminded that they are interrupting or disturbing other people's work. Children are asked to move about quietly and in a restrained manner, and soon accept this as normal behaviour. In fact children tend to move independently and individually. Whole classes no longer stand up together and place chairs under tables simultaneously as often happens in the traditional classroom. Visitors to open plan schools frequently remark on the level of noise which is often less than occurs in a classroom.

Standards of tidiness too are usually higher. Again because facilities are shared there has to be agreement about putting things away tidily and replacing them in the places where they were found. Checking of apparatus becomes second nature to children brought up in this way. Open shelving also imposes tidiness where there are no doors to hide muddles.

The larger numbers involved also mean that there is a greater variety of individual quirks of behaviour to be encountered. Children learn of necessity, therefore, to live together, to tolerate one another's idiosyncrasies and to give and take. Consideration for others is the rule. Upsets do occur and tempers become frayed but the greater space provided by the open plan structure allows incompatibles to be dispersed and diverted more easily. Children have the benefit in open plan units of seeing adults working together and cooperating with one another. They quickly follow the example set and reflect the attitudes of their elders in their own behaviour. It seems reasonable to assume that standards of social behaviour ought in fact to be higher in open plan schools.

Aesthetic standards also might well be more stringent. It has already been indicated that display is often of a high standard; probably as suggested by a teacher the other day, 'One is kept on one's toes because one's work is on view at all times'. This was not said with any thought of competition in her mind, but simply in answer to comments about the high standards demonstrated. There is a desire in such a school to do one's best – a very healthy attitude and much preferred to the atmosphere of competition prevalent in some classrooms where children may be heard comparing their own and others' achievements. 'I'm on book 4 – you're only on book 2' is the sort of hurtful comment made. In the well-run open plan school children are encouraged by the attitude and example of the teacher to improve on their own previous efforts – to compete with themselves, not with others – and where display is concerned to cooperate with one another in producing something pleasing.

As with social and aesthetic standards, intellectual standards depend on the attitudes of the teachers. It has already been said that the open plan situation can be beneficial to the inexperienced or inexpert teacher because she is able to see how her more experienced and more capable colleagues perform.

The headteacher may in discussion with staff lay down general aims and objectives to be attempted. Teachers will, however, recognize that some individuals may never be able to reach these general goals and will encourage each child simply to do his best. It should be recognized, however, that each individual can improve his performance. Frequently teachers' expectations of certain children are too low and standards consequently suffer. Even in the old traditional grammar school for which the top 25 per cent of children were normally selected under the old 11+ examination, and in which children tended to be streamed according to ability, teachers of the lowest stream have been heard to complain 'What can you do with a shower like this?', quite forgetting that these children were more able (in terms of the examination) than the top stream of the secondary modern school. Because little was expected of those pupils their performance deteriorated. Sometimes the primary school teacher falls into a similar trap with comparable results.

This is probably less likely to happen in the open plan situation where a number of teachers work together. Other teachers might recognize that a child is under-achieving because of a colleague's low expectations and advise her accordingly. Or the child himself might find another teacher's attitude more encouraging and gravitate towards that member of staff. There is certainly opportunity for staff to share their observations and assessment of all the children in the unit and, therefore, less probability of any child's potential being underestimated. There is also less opportunity, in a shared work area where more adults are available to supervize, for children to opt out of the learning situation.

Each child's capabilities should be recognized and his progress rewarded. He should be encouraged to put in maximum effort and to do his best. At the same time teachers must recognize that children develop in fits and starts, and that growth in all areas (see Plowden Report) happens in spurts and plateaus. Children need time to consolidate learning and indeed time to relax. As adults, we do not always read books of intellectual value which will extend our knowledge: we read for enjoyment and relaxation as well. So do children. As teachers, therefore, we must recognize that children cannot be expected to work at full stretch all the time. We must try to provide for the immediate needs of each individual at any given time. This presents an almost super-human task and can only be done by keeping adequate records of each individual (see Chapter 6).

Good records depend upon observation and the sensitivity of the teacher. A common complaint made by teachers who are encouraged to observe children more closely is that there is insufficient time to do so. They feel obliged to spend all their time teaching facts and skills and do not seem to recognize that their teaching would probably be more effective if they made time to observe what their children say and do.

For instance a teacher had in her class a boy of five-plus who had been in school for two terms. His home background was unsatisfactory and his father in prison. Older children from this family had not done particularly well. Expectations for this child were understandably low. He appeared to lack concentration and to drift rather aimlessly from one occupation to another. However, his teacher, who was sensitive and extremely capable, suspected that she might be underestimating him and felt that she ought to observe the child more closely to see whether there was any pattern in his learning behaviour. She started him off on a number activity first thing in the morning and then watched him unobtrusively throughout the session. He completed the task she had given him which involved counting, and then wandered over to a display on a religious theme to which everyone in the class was contributing from time to time. Here he counted the number of people depicted in a crowd scene and then went to draw two or three more people, coloured them in crayon, cut them out and added them to the frieze. He then traced the background of hills with his finger and came to the teacher to ask what hills were made of — were they made of stones? This school is situated in a particularly flat part of the country and hills were not part of this child's personal experience. They talked about the height of hills and the difficulty people have in climbing the rocky surfaces. Then the boy went off to the sand tray where he began to make hills and valleys to which he added some specimen rocks from the discovery table. Other children joined him and he explained what he was doing. Finally he placed shells, used for counting, up and down his hills to represent people, ending up by counting the shells and telling his companions how many 'people' there were. Contrary to expectation then the teacher discovered that this child was following a definite train of thought, relating his number knowledge to other situations, seeking

110

information and acting upon it. At the end of the morning the teacher had a much better understanding of the child and his ability, and was able to plan his personal programme much more effectively.

The impression might have been given erroneously that this teacher did nothing else all morning but watch Peter. She was, of course, following her usual pattern of helping the children generally but kept a particularly sharp eye on this particular boy from time to time and talked to him about what he was doing. In the teacher's opinion the time was well spent because it gave her a better insight into the needs of this particular child. This teacher always attempted to give equal care to all her children, and when more time and attention was spent on some children, compensated by giving extra time to others on subsequent days.

In order to keep abreast of each child's needs and development teachers must make time for observation and discussion. It is easier to do this in a situation such as that described in Chapter 2, where children can be purposefully employed on a variety of activities, thus allowing the teacher to withdraw a child or a group for a specific teaching purpose. The open plan school is purpose-built to provide ideal conditions for this kind of approach, and because there are more teachers available and able to pool observations and make shared assessments of each child, expectations are likely to be more accurate. If the needs of individual children are recognized and met in the ways described, it follows that intellectual standards overall should be higher. Ultimately, in the open plan school, as in any other type of school, standards depend entirely on the enthusiasm, knowledge and expertise of the teachers and the learning environment which they provide.

8 Planning the curriculum

In recent years most primary schools have ceased to teach subjects in isolated compartments, and the basic skills of language and numeracy are taught alongside other subjects. Rigid syllabuses are less frequently seen now, and teachers have a great deal of freedom to effect children's learning through their needs and interests. Broad educational aims (such as 'the education of each individual to his full potential') have long since replaced the narrow requirements of the old elementary schools. Perhaps the aims of primary education have become too vague, so that they are open to misunderstanding by observers or by less experienced teachers. There are many today who are demanding a more rigorous study of the aims and objectives of primary education, and teachers in open plan schools need to consider their priorities carefully if they are not to be accused of vague and woolly idealism.

One of the many vague concepts is that of child-centred education which replaced the teacher-directed work of the elementary schools in accordance with the ideas of psychologists and specialists in child development. Inevitably, the term 'child-centred education' has led to a misunderstanding of the role of the teacher. Experienced teachers will know that it is very far from the truth to consider a child-centred learning situation as one where teachers abdicate their responsibilities so that children learn by expressing themselves freely. Indeed, the newer kind of teaching is much more demanding on the adult, requiring her to provide the necessary stimulating environment within which a child has some choice (necessarily limited) of activities. This is a very skilled task, and it is analysed more fully in Chapter 7. In essence, the teacher's role in an open plan school is to provide an environment which will cause children to learn — 'learning-centred' seems to be a more useful label here than 'child-centred'. In addition to all the varied day-to-day tasks that this entails, learning-centred education demands that the teacher becomes an expert planner of learning experiences. She is required not only to know her children and the psychology of their development, but also to assess her objectives and ensure that the children make progress.

Schemes of work
Many schools have abandoned tight timetables with clear subject categories, and sometimes this has tended to lead to the abandonment of a

112

structuring of the work to be covered, so that each teacher is responsible for her own schemes and syllabus as well as for the timing of the activities. But there is a basic duty for all the staff of a school to provide for a continuity in the children's learning, and a progression of experiences. A teacher in any school – open plan or conventional – should not work so independently of her colleagues that children repeat work as they go up the school, or that large gaps are left. All teachers know of children who have repeated the same topic year after year (e.g. frog-spawn and tadpoles every Spring). This is not to say that there is no value in a child repeating aspects of his studies, provided that there is a planned deepening or widening of the concepts and not merely a hit-or-miss repetition without progression.

A headteacher should provide schemes of work which will make for continuity and progression, but which will also allow a large amount of freedom for the teachers. This is not difficult to do in the more linear subjects – mathematics, for example – but activities such as environmental studies are not easy to structure so that progression is maintained. Many headteachers tackle this problem by having a member of staff who is the school 'consultant' or 'adviser' (not specialist teacher) on a particular aspect of the curriculum (see Chapters 6 and 7). The head and teacher will consult with colleagues in a 'working party' relationship in order to plan schemes in the activity or subject for the whole school. This might also be discussed with other schools in the catchment area so that there is continuity throughout the child's schooling from five to sixteen – many a first-year pupil in a secondary school has been dismayed to find that he begins yet again in history with cavemen and the stone age.

Once produced, a school's scheme of work should not become static and inflexible. It can be changed as teachers contribute new ideas, and it can be interpreted liberally. Teachers need not consider the headteacher's syllabus to be a divine tablet. Indeed it has been well said that a scheme is like a route or a map – the teacher knows where the work is leading and what the goal is to be, but this need not prevent the children from seeking interesting byways and following unexpected developments, provided the teacher can set them on course again when she thinks it necessary.

It is stated above that schemes for linear subjects such as mathematics can be easier to construct than for subjects where there is no clear progression. The acquisition of reading skills is another important activity which is usually considered to be one which can be planned to allow for steady progression. Nevertheless, there is much controversy about the structuring of mathematical and language learning. There are now many courses, schemes and programmes available for learning the basic subjects, and most schools invest funds in them. In attempting to educate children as individuals, teachers often set children to work at appropriate places in published schemes or courses and then watch their progress through the graded tasks. But working through a reading scheme or mathematics programme is no substitute for the wise guidance of teachers: as textbooks have sometimes dictated the courses in secondary schools, so there is a danger of published materials controlling the work in some primary schools. Schemes and programmes are published to help teachers and not to determine the curriculum. Similarly television and radio broadcasts are available to enrich the curriculum, or to provide starting points, but not to dictate the work. It is the teacher's ability to be selective for her children that is crucial. This is not to state that a reading scheme, for example, is of little value — indeed, much of the material is excellent and teachers are often wise to use a scheme as a framework for this important part of the curriculum. But a tedious groping through a scheme can also be inhibiting and frustrating for the children: there must be a wealth of support material, parallel schemes and a wise guidance of children through the various alternatives.

Most schools make careful plans for continuity of work in the basic subjects and relate other activities to the development of language and mathematics. Even so, every teacher will know that children do not always progress steadily: there are occasional 'plateau periods' and even regressions at times. Indeed, we are told by psychologists that concepts are not acquired in a steady sequence, but they grow and are modified throughout our lives. Thus a child may return again and again to study the same idea but at a deeper or wider level each time. A simple example will make this obvious: an infant will play with an electric torch and understand the use of the switch to turn it on and off; a junior child can come to understand the circuitry involved and go on to make parallel and series circuits; the secondary child will progress to Ohm's Law ... and so on. The same learning process takes place in other subjects: a historical concept is added to as the child grows — no pupil has ever 'done the Romans' once and for all. This basic understanding of how children learn profoundly affects our curriculum planning, for how, to continue with historical concepts, can history be taught chronologically through the primary years when we know that sequential learning in this way is not psychologically sound? Even so, many junior schools still keep to a conventional history syllabus — cavemen, Greeks and Romans for the first year, Middle Ages for the second year, and so on: many secondary schools then repeat the process.

The problem, put simply, is how can a school provide for continuity and progression of learning without denying a child the opportunity to repeat work and experiences at deeper or wider levels? How can a scheme be undogmatic and liberal without at the same time leading to a woolly or hit-or-miss selection of experiences? The problem is made more difficult because the ordered acquisition of knowledge seems irrelevant when there can be no agreement about what the essential historical, geographical or scientific concepts are that a child must study by the age of eleven.

So, in non-linear, general subjects, it is not possible to determine what knowledge is of most value to every child. But this does not mean that any curriculum will do. Recent thinking about educational objectives has been showing how curricula may be planned not only by their content of knowledge, but also by the skills to be mastered and the values, attitudes and interests to be fostered.

'With objectives in mind'

In most schools, schemes of work are lists of content with little reference to why a course is planned in a certain way or what the teachers are teaching if for. Presumably there are certain understood objectives in the minds of the teachers: the courses perhaps are designed to teach children skills or factual knowledge, or to affect attitudes and values. But any course aught first to specify what objectives a teacher has in mind. Indeed, planning for a course should contain two lists; first the objectives state what the course is aiming to achieve, second the list of content matter (perhaps in a flow diagram) shows how the objectives are to reached.

Now objectives are far more specific than general aims. For example, an aim of an environmental studies course might be 'to enable every child to gain some understanding of his own environment'. This is worthy enough, but it is vague and indefinite; it is more a declaration of intent than a description of precise objectives. The teacher here would need to give clear definitions of the objectives needed to reach the aim, and a list of learning experiences to attain the objectives. But defining the objectives for a course is not easy for teachers who have customarily been offered as the only guide a list of subject-matter which has to be covered in a year. Fortunately, a great deal of thought and study has been given in recent years to the defining of curriculum objectives, and this work is now influencing the planning of courses in primary schools.

Two Schools Council projects in particular are, by listing objectives, giving some structure to important areas of the primary school curriculum. These are areas (science, history, geography, social science) where it has been extremely difficult to specify content-matter or in what order the content should be taught.

'Science 5–13' is a project that has produced a number of books which comprise units of work. The units are linked by matching a child's stage of development to the appropriate activities, and both of these are affected by an awareness of the objectives involved.

Knowledge of the child's stage of development

Knowledge of objectives and activities suited to various stages of development

Activities matching the child's stage of development

(From 'With objectives in mind' *Guide to Science 5–13*, published for the Schools Council by Macdonald Educational.)

The objectives are listed in detail under the following headings:

attitudes, interests and aesthetic awareness
observing, exploring and ordering observation
developing basic concepts and logical thinking
posing questions and devising experiments or investigations to answer them
acquiring knowledge and learning skills
communicating
appreciating patterns and relationships
interpreting findings critically

The second project, which has yet to produce its final report, is 'History, Geography and Social Science 8–13', defined by its director (Professor W. A. L. Blyth) as having 'something to do with history, geography, economics, sociology, anthropology, social psychology and political science'. In brief, the study is of man in place, time and society. This project does not aim to provide packs of materials for use in schools because teachers, schools and the children's backgrounds differ: 'eight year olds in a multiracial area of a large city might need very different materials from those which might make an impact on eleven year olds in a remote rural area or a highpriced suburb'. Instead, the project is diffusing its ideas in a few selected areas and preparing a range of publications which will help teachers in their curriculum planning.

The project lists its objectives, headed 'Skills to be mastered' and 'Attitudes, values and interests to be fostered', and they are concerned with intellectual, social and physical skills in the first list and personal qualities in the second. Teachers who have used these lists of objectives have found them very useful in planning their courses. Another element which could prove to be of value to those who are unsure what to include in history or geography and other courses is that concerned with key concepts. In brief, the project team has tried to draw up a list of the concepts which are central to an understanding of man in time, place and society. The seven key concepts are: communication, power, values and beliefs, conflict/consensus, continuity/change, similarity/difference and causality. All these relate fundamentally to the subject-matter of history, geography and social sciences, and again teachers have reported that they found them useful in planning and executing units of study within their courses.

Also of great value could be the project's concern with social science, for our traditional curriculum has usually neglected the community aspects of our environment. There is much exciting work in environmental studies to be seen in primary schools, but the project's attempt to communicate the ideas of social scientists to older juniors could add an important dimension to teaching.

There are other projects aimed at helping teachers to plan their curriculum, but the two mentioned above could give a lead in helping teachers to match the syllabuses to their objectives. This requires a rigorous examination of what schools are trying to do. When a piece of work has been completed, it is important to assess whether the objectives have been reached. It is easy enough to apply tests to see if factual knowledge has been acquired, but it will be a far more difficult business to decide whether or not the work has led to the attainment of objectives. But evaluation of the objectives and learning experiences is essential if we wish to know how effective our teaching has been. In open plan schools, the evaluating will often be made by the teaching team discussing successes and failures. This could be done by means, not only of tests, but by recording the responses and attitudes of the individual children as they are observed. These observations will affect the planning of future work. Indeed, the development of the curriculum is best seen as a cyclical progression from aims and objectives to assessments and evaluation, with a subsequent rethinking of objectives as necessary:

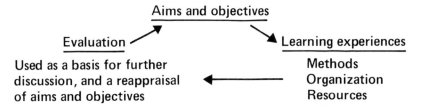

This kind of rigorous scrutiny of the curriculum is not easy to do. But open plan schools demand rigour from teachers and children: anything less could deservedly earn the attacks frequently heard that modern educational methods are woolly, vague and impractical. Open plan schools should be places which establish a reputation for their high quality of teaching and learning, and thorough curriculum planning, which brings together theory and practice, is vital for this.

Integration and interrelation of subjects
Although it is rarely asked at what age children can be ready to learn in subjects, it is generally assumed that the curriculum should be integrated in primary schools and that subject teaching by specialists should begin in secondary schools. Be that as it may, primary schools, with their general, nonspecialist teachers, are able to abandon the watertight compartmentalization of subjects and integrate the work around themes, topics and projects. Designers of new schools have responded to integrated ways of working, and this has had a considerable influence on the building of open plan schools which give excellent opportunities for this approach.

It would be tedious to repeat the wellknown advantages of integration, but one aspect does deserve comment. This is that a traditional curriculum can be very inhibiting. Professor Blyth has implied that sociology, anthropology, social psychology and political science can all be involved in a topic for upper juniors as well as the traditional history and geography. A popular topic such as weather studies can involve physics, statistics, ecology as well as meteorology. Indeed, there is hardly an aspect of human knowledge that young children *at their level* cannot find of interest. And this in itself is a justification for abandoning the tight subject timetable.

Whatever the course being planned, there will be links with other aspects of the curriculum. Environmental studies, for example, will develop language skills (factual recording, purposeful discussion, creative expression, the use of books), aesthetic awareness (collecting and displaying, appreciation of the qualities of material things, perceiving what they would fail to see without a teacher's guidance) as well as the acquisition of knowledge (collecting, grouping, classifying information, developing concepts of direction, scale, distance, time). So a topic within an environmental studies scheme could embrace history, science, language, mathematics, art and social science as well as geography. For example, a local canal studied in a school could embrace all these subjects and many others.

This is not an argument for dispensing with subjects as academic disciplines. Indeed, if we asked what adult historians, geographers, or scientists actually do, we might find that young children could pursue these disciplines at their level. For example, a geographer studies, among other things, an environment, and tries to synthesize the many observed facts so that he can build up a complete picture and interpret the relationship between the inhabitants and the environment. A child can do this too in the neighbourhood of his school or home, and he can make records just like an adult geographer (in writing, sketches, photographs, maps). A historian, like a detective, attempts to interpret items of evidence; young children can examine their old school logbook and try to understand the lives of schoolchildren a hundred years ago. This could be a richer historical experience for children than rushing through centuries of history in a chronological syllabus (although history must include the stories and myths of our heritage). Scientists observe, record and hypothesize; young children can do this too.

This means that not only are subjects linked together, but also that young children can enjoy the subjects in themselves, provided that teachers fully understand what the subjects really are and how they are studied. The Schools Council project 'History, Geography and Social Science 8–13' referred to sees academic subjects as resources from which the teacher draws in order to enrich the topics: 'Each academic discipline should be valued for its distinctive skills and content and approach, but should be complemented by the others, in the achievement of objectives during the middle years.' Subjects are interrelated so that they contribute to the solution of a problem or the pursuit of a theme or topic.

Assignments

The development of 'the integrated day' has led to the use of assignment systems in schools. This often means that children have quite long periods in which to complete a number of tasks set by the teacher. An observer in a modern primary school today will be sure to see children working at their tasks, not only from graded schemes and reference books but also from assignment cards prepared by the teacher. The purpose of a work or assignment card is to give individual children or a small group a piece of work that will further their development. As all the children are different, this may mean that a card is prepared for the use of only one child; it may be designed to help him master a difficulty that he has met in the scheme, or it may be to extend his thinking beyond what the scheme has allowed for. Assignment cards should never be mass-produced and used over and over again like textbooks.

Sometimes a unit of study may be centred around a set of cards made by the teacher. The cards will form only a core, for not all the children will work right through the set. In some cases, slower children will have to be supplied with additional cards, or brighter children will work with cards which point to researches to be conducted or references to be sought in books. With the topic completed by the children, the cards will have come to the end of their usefulness. Unlike textbooks, they can then be thrown away. If it should happen that the teacher wishes to use the cards again he would, as curriculum development theorists recommend, analyse and evaluate their success before removing some of the cards or adding new ones to the set.

In one existing open plan school which makes good use of assignment cards, there is a relationship between the cards and all the other resources in the school. This is a school for about eighty children (twenty-five infants and fifty-five juniors) with three teachers, one of whom is the headmaster.

Each area has sets of cards which are constantly being evaluated and renewed. The cards cover mathematics, language, cooking and topic work. The language cards include some published materials (e.g. Stott's kit) as well as cards which contain stories that children may also hear on the cassette recorder. The mathematics cards are based upon a scheme prepared by a working party of the authority's teachers; they call for the use of all kinds of materials and equipment as well as for published sources. The mathematics cards are adapted as necessary to the needs of individual children, and any unit in the curriculum which includes some mathematical aspects will have cards specifically prepared for it.

The work in the school is at the individual level where necessary, with children working either from a set of cards, or from cards specially prepared for the child, or from published schemes and kits. In all cases, the needs of the child determine the curriculum, and the cards are provided to help the development of the work, not to dictate the curriculum. There is the subtle but profound difference between one teaching situation where

Figure 34

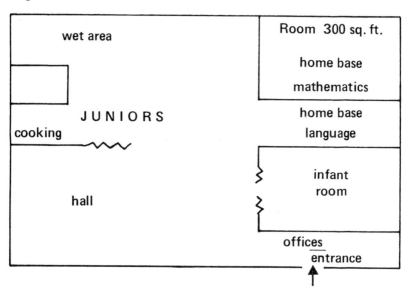

the child follows the cards or textbook regardless of his needs, abilities and interests, and a situation where a wise teacher uses his judgement to guide the child to the right task or equipment or card that the child needs.

The spaces in this school are carefully organized for this individual approach. The hall is timetabled for only four half-days, so that each teaching group can have its periods for PE, television broadcasts, music and so on. At these times the screens are closed. For the rest of the week the hall is a large space where children can work at their assignments and topics. The enclosable room in the junior section is used as a home base and also for mathematics; it can quickly be made available without any great difficulty for either of the two junior groups for class work. The infant space is basically a well-equipped classroom, except that children may spill into the hall for much of the week.

A great deal of work has had to go into the making of assignment cards used in this particular school, but they have been assembled over a period of time, and the three teachers have shared the work by mutual agreement. In larger teams of teachers, there may have to be some organization of the tasks, so that the teachers contribute fairly to the general good of the team. A team's 'adviser' in a particular subject will probably determine, through discussion, the general development of assignment systems, and plan in detail the design of the schemes. Then there has to be consultation about the siting of the various cards in the available spaces. In Chapter 7 it can be seen how a learning environment is created by teachers who organize resources so that children know where to go for materials, books and work cards. Indeed, it is the organization and disposition of everyday resources such as scissors, pencils, brushes, paper, books and the like that will enable an open plan school to function smoothly. Things must be available, catalogued and organized in an orderly fashion in familiar places so that children may have access to them without difficulty or fuss.

In the school shown in Figure 34, the three teachers believe in high standards of presentation. Even a 'one off' work card is made attractive. This is done by careful printing of the text, by the use of different coloured papers mounted on to the basic card and by careful layout of the material. It is justifiably argued by the headteacher that the high standards set by the teachers have a profound influence on the work which the children do.

The 'hidden' curriculum

A thoughtfully-planned curriculum, with its lists of objectives and content-matter, with its carefully produced assignment and work cards, with its well-planned integration of subjects and organization of spaces, can still fail to produce a happy, industrious school. Every educational institution has a concealed curriculum which exists independently of what the teachers are overtly planning. This hidden curriculum is one that affects children through the human relationships within the school. All the effort put into curriculum planning will be negated if the relationships, values and attitudes in the school are not right. Pupils respond to each other and to their teachers as people, and every curriculum succeeds or fails according to the relationships which establish the ethos of the school. The question of human relationships and the hidden curriculum are more important in open plan schools than in others because groups of children and adults come together more in both formal and informal situations. The behaviour of people towards each other in these situations has more effect on the children than the most rigorously planned curriculum.

References

SCHOOLS COUNCIL (1972) *Science 5/13 Project* London: Macdonald Educational

SCHOOLS COUNCIL (1972) *History, Geography and Social Science 8–13* London: Schools Council

9 The school and the community

Too often home and school pull in different directions. Many parents consider school to be an institution for furthering a child's life opportunities, and academic attainment is the main criterion. Many teachers – and especially those who choose to teach in open plan schools, or are dedicated to the principles of modern education – see education as the development of the child's whole personality to the limit of his potential. This is not to say that academic standards are forgotten by teachers in open plan schools: indeed, a main argument in this book is that the children's individual work in the new schools can and should lead to higher intellectual achievement. Nevertheless, there is often a misunderstanding on the part of parents about what goes on inside school, and this chapter considers the importance of bringing parents and teachers together in the interests of the children.

Home problems which children bring to school with them
Many children come to school with a burden of problems that they have to live with at home. In a conventional classroom a sensitive teacher will become aware of the difficult lives of some of the pupils and will give help where he can. In open plan schools where a team of teachers is working with a large group of children it could happen that a child's problems might go undetected or be misunderstood in some situations. On the other hand, it sometimes happens that another teacher, not the child's own class teacher, will become aware of the child's problems and will discuss them with colleagues. Certainly, open plan schools must not neglect the importance of the teacher's pastoral work with the child. An experienced teacher will know how a child's problems at home can affect his school life and his development, but for the less-experienced reader it is perhaps worth considering the main difficulties which too many children live with.

There is ample evidence that social class differences affect children's education. Bernstein has shown how the linguistic backgrounds of children influence intellectual development, and Douglas's researches published in *The Home and the School* emphasize the importance of the parents' concern for their children's education (Douglas 1964):

At both eight and eleven years, but particularly at eleven, the highest average scores in the tests are made by children whose parents are interested in their education, and the lowest by those whose parents are least interested. This is partly a social class effect stemming from the large proportion of upper middle-class children among the former and of manual working-class children among the latter.

However, Bernstein and Douglas, and many others, appear to be mainly concerned with the effect of the home background on children's intellectual performance at school. There are, of course, also certain home pressures that will affect not only a child's intellectual attainments, but also his whole personality.

Normally, children will have attained a certain amount of independence by the age of seven. Also, if well developed, they will have established satisfactory relationships with other people.

But a child's success in living happily alongside other people will depend on a balancing of opposing tensions. On the one hand, he needs the security of a loving home and caring school, yet on the other hand he needs the opportunity to achieve his own independence and autonomy. An over-emphasis on security without a balancing opportunity to attain autonomy could warp a child's development. Parents have the difficult task of maintaining the balance. They should not, for example, smother a child's initiative and do everything for him when he is capable of doing some things for himself. Neither should parents give a young child so much freedom and independence that he feels insecure and neglected. A balance, too, must be maintained between a child's natural wish to rebel against his elders at times, and his desire to cooperate and be accepted. Again, the child's egotism should be balanced by giving him opportunities to show kindness and unselfishness. One of the more difficult balances to maintain is that between the development of a child's own sense of standards and the necessary acceptance of other people's differing standards and life styles. Tolerance and freedom from prejudice are not attitudes which are easily acquired in some homes.

A home which manages to balance these and other conflicting aspects of a child's nature will allow a seven or eight year old to enjoy one of the happiest periods of his life. But a junior school child can become frustrated and even maladjusted if he has failed to develop well in earlier years. By the age of eight or nine a child is needing less protection at home, and he is looking outwards to establish more permanent relationships with his peers. He is anxious to be accepted by the friendship groups within his class and in the playground. Child guidance clinics help many junior school children who should be enjoying what is often said to be the 'golden age of childhood', but whose anxieties and frustrations, which have their origins in the children's homes, have led to behaviour problems.

Successful parenthood is not easy. The care of children can be mismanaged in any kind of home, the poor or the affluent, the ignorant or

the educated. Every primary school teacher has children from broken homes, and these children are nearly always cared for and treated kindly at school. Perhaps it is less often realized that the apparently warm, secure and even affluent home can sometimes make for an unbalanced upbringing which can warp a child's growth.

There are mothers who cannot discipline themselves enough to allow the right balance of security and autonomy for their children – they find it easier to give way to the child's demands rather than to insist on more reasonable behaviour. Thus a child can be over-indulged and spoilt, and by eight or nine years he may be showing off and wanting his own way in school, while at the same time be trying to get on with his companions. The tensions may be too much for the child who feels inferior and perhaps resorts to bullying or stealing or some other form of unwelcome behaviour.

Sometimes the spoilt child is from a home where the mother is anxious not to let the child out of her sight. Most headteachers are familiar with such parents who harass both the child and the school in their unreasonable anxiety for the child. This kind of mother will breed nervousness in the child, and by showing too much love and emotion, without at the same time giving some independence, she is doing harm to the person she so much cares for.

It often happens that the love for the child is a warped version of a mother's self-love: she – or often he, the father – is trying to fulfil the parent's own ambitions in the child. 11+ success is wanted at home so that the child can make up for all that the parents did not have. For many children, this sort of strain leads to anxiety and even to severe mental or physical ill-health: children are simply required to take on too great a load of responsibility for their years, and the burden is overwhelming. Most teachers will know adults – even perhaps colleagues in the profession – who are ashamed of their failure at a selective examination in their primary school years, but who have managed to overcome the feeling of inferiority. There must be many more citizens who never really throw off unwarranted shame because their parents failed to show sympathy and understanding while demanding too much of a child.

A family's attitudes can affect a child's development and way of life. So much of a child's growth to maturity is dependent upon the examples he has to imitate and the early experiences he has been offered. Homes therefore which show undesirable attitudes to other people do not help the child to develop healthy social attitudes. Some homes show no care for the special needs of the elderly or the sick, others ignore or even mock incapacities or handicaps. Even the children themselves are subject to ridicule in some homes where their immature language or stammering or slowness is a subject for family criticism or even derision. Again, a family's attitudes to people of different races and skin colour are absorbed by the children and ultimately affect their beliefs and way of life.

The mobility of families today has often broken up the extended families of a close village or town community. There is no granny or aunty round the corner when a young couple and their baby go to live on a new estate. Sometimes, families develop an unhealthy exclusiveness. The family unit looks in upon itself, nobody else is wanted and nothing else matters. It is not unknown for young married teachers, who are among the poorer classes of our society, to live in neighbourhoods which they would not choose if they had more wealth. They worry about their own children's development in an undesirable part of town, especially when the children pick up the unwelcome speech habits of the area very quickly. For such families it is not always easy to prevent exclusiveness developing. The challenge is to be friendly with neighbours and still preserve one's own different standards. But children are judging the behaviour of others well before they come to school. They meet different patterns of speech and behaviour and they play with children of many different backgrounds. They do not necessarily suffer harm by assimilating themselves with different kinds of friendship groups and they quickly adapt and change their speech patterns. This is not to say that it is easy to bring up children to retain the family's own high standards without at the same time avoiding exclusiveness and learning tolerance for others.

A good home, then, is one where a child can learn sympathy and concern for others. It is one which does not exhibit unhealthy prejudices about other people or customs, and it tolerates diversity while balancing this with a retention of its own sense of standards. Our pupils in school would, only too often, be happier and more successful if more parents were aware of the effect of their own beliefs on their children's social development.

There are unsatisfactory homes of many different kinds. Some are too solemn and serious, where there is no friendly teasing, no natural laughter or sense of proportion. Some set no example of the moral virtues of truth or honesty or justice; the children never learn the importance of taking their turn and of recognizing other people's needs. The material values of a society where 'keeping up with the Jones's' is the mark of success will also affect children. Do parents value possessions because they are expensive, beautiful, or simply better than their neighbours? Does the home have to be kept so spotlessly clean that normal living in it becomes almost impossible? For children of such families, *things* come to matter more than *people.* It is not unknown for children of such homes to grow up and try to redress the balance themselves, so that they become the destroyers of property rather than the preservers of it. Children need to grow with a respect for material things, but not with an obsessive lust for acquisition.

A diminishing number of parents today reject education. Nevertheless, there are still those who have no respect for learning or the arts. Worthwhile activities are considered highbrow, and labels such as 'egghead' or 'square' are used. Some parents can be of no help to the child in guiding his future. In a society where winning a football pool competition is the gateway to paradise, there must be children who are growing up to have no pleasure or zest in their work, and for whom all problems could be solved by a lucky win. In this respect, as in so many others, teachers have the probably impossible task of redressing the balance in an economic system which has been rapidly moving away from one in which a person's home life and work could coexist harmoniously. For too many, life begins when they leave the factory gates.

In summary, a child at home imbibes the values, ideas, attitudes and purposes of his family. His development can be affected in so far as he is set bad examples. He wants to be one of the group (sending to bed for bad behaviour is hated when it means leaving the group atmosphere), and he needs to adjust himself to the standards of the group. Sometimes the standards may be undesirable in some of the ways we have indicated. But this is not to say that the child's development will inevitably be warped or damaged. A child can suffer many of the disadvantages of a bad home, or even of the death of parents, and still become a stable, adjusted personality. Indeed, the teaching profession itself contains many who struggled to attain education in spite of the indifference, or even the hostility, of their families. It is worth noting that the profession of elementary school teaching was originally one of the very few ladders upon which a working-class child from the slums of a big town could climb to a better life.

So, although a high proportion of maladjusted children come from bad homes, it is by no means the case that a child is necessarily harmed for life because some things are wrong at home. But teachers should, at least, be aware of the difficulties which many children face. No school – open plan or not – should ignore the home background of its pupils. Indeed, the school should go beyond this and try positively to improve the lot of their pupils at home by helping the parents to understand the needs of growing children.

This task imposes a number of problems. Some disturbed children are able to conceal problems which would overwhelm other children, and teachers have to use all their skills to give help where it is not always obvious to see the need. A few parents will resist all attempts by the teachers to enter into a partnership with the school. In any staffroom there may be inexperienced teachers who are themselves facing the problems of earning their own livelihood for the first time, or have had little experience of young children or of modern teaching methods. Yet primary schools have a long record of providing pastoral care for their children. Chapter 3 emphasizes the need for teachers to establish secure relationships with children, and an open plan should not allow the necessary stability to suffer. The new schools must retain the best of primary school traditions for the care of the pupils, and it is of vital importance that the systems of team teaching and cooperation between teachers, described elsewhere in this book, should not endanger the basic happy atmosphere that exists in so many infant and junior schools.

Teachers and parents

For many years elementary schools were built with high walls around their playgrounds. The walls emphasized the special nature of the school and demarcated its sphere of influence in the community. Even in the middle of a busy town the schools were isolated from life around them, and the walls safeguarded the pupils cocooned within their island fortress of education and culture. There was some interchange with life outside the school, and parents were even allowed within the walls on special occasions.

Schools are very different places today, and parents are encouraged to become involved in the education of their children. The Plowden Report on 'Children and their Primary Schools' (1967) emphasized the importance of encouraging parents to cooperate in the work of the school, and many teachers have found ways and means of including the parents in the general life of the school.

The new open plan schools may encounter suspicion and resistance from parents. Some of them, encouraged by unfavourable articles in the press, look upon the new schools as places where free activity goes unchecked and where low educational standards are the result. Others have been misled by the phrase 'open plan', and they think of a situation where far too many children are thrown together to the discomfiture of all. There are probably no parents at present who themselves went to an open plan school, and they will naturally be wary of something outside their direct experience.

Teachers have a fundamental duty to explain the aims of the school to the parents and to prove to them that very high standards are attainable. There are many ways of 'selling' the school to bewildered parents, and teachers are familiar with the standard methods. Parent-teacher organizations can be of great value when the headteacher gives the necessary leadership. Annual or termly parental visits to school functions are encouraged, and the parents' evening, when teachers interview parents by a rota, are a familiar institution in many schools.

But PTA meetings and parents' evenings are mainly formal functions which may not convey the school's ideals to the anxious mothers and fathers. More flexible and open ways of breaking down the barriers between school and home are needed.

An interesting innovation in recent years has been the construction of community schools in which the building has been designed to accommodate the neighbourhood's children as well as people from other age groups. A coffee bar, recreation rooms, a library and lounges may be included in the building, and parents and others are welcome to use them during the school day. As activities for the adults develop there is opportunity for parents, children and teachers to meet at school and work together. At times the community facilities in the building are free and available for the children, so relieving pressure on teaching accommodation. In the evenings the community spaces in the school are available for the various group and club activities which take place in a community, and games such as badminton can be held in the school hall. Often, though, it is desirable to enclose the pupils' teaching areas so that work may be left undisturbed by evening activities – many teachers have suffered in our old schools from evening meetings which left children's precious models and displays damaged by groups badly controlled by their leaders. Purpose-built community schools need headteachers and staff who are truly interested in the community, and who are willing to involve themselves in activities which are far wider in scope than the traditional work of a primary school. The headteacher in particular adds another sphere to his duties for he will, certainly in the first instance when the school is new, have to welcome many visitors to his school and to liaise with various community workers and leaders.

But the majority of new primary schools do not have purpose-built community spaces and resources, and the staff have to make contact with parents without the benefit of special facilities. Many headteachers have pioneered new attitudes to parents and notices saying 'No parents beyond this point' are becoming rare today. In some schools mothers visit regularly with their pre-school age children, who are gradually introduced to school life before they even enter as pupils (see Chapter 3). Sometimes statutory regulations are stretched so that young children attend for some half-days before they are officially on the register as pupils. The loneliness of mothers at home all day with young children is recognized by social workers, and some schools now do a great deal to help these parents. The mothers perhaps come to school for coffee mornings: sometimes a group of mothers (and fathers too) will have a lunch at school with their children, and a rota scheme is organized so that two or three parents dine with the children every day. In a few schools parents extend the idea of eating with the children by running the school 'cafe' in a spare room, where infants come for their morning milk and snack. For this the children are given pleasant cups and saucers and sit at table. For the children from deprived homes especially this method of taking school milk gives a far higher sense of standards than the all too frequent method of distribution. One of the more unpleasant sights in junior schools used to be the clutter of broken straws and battered milk-bottle tops scattered in a classroom where the teacher had a low sense of standards.

The effort to improve links with the community is sometimes organized methodically on a regular basis. Swimming, for example, could become an activity for children – and their parents – after normal school hours, and other junior school activities such as cookery and pottery could be run on an after-school basis, with volunteer teachers and parents organizing the work. At least one school has experimented with a flexible, staggered day, so that some members of staff arrive late in the morning and stay to run late-afternoon activities after the end of the normal school day. This innovation would, of course, require the cooperation of the local authority. The statutory regulations requiring a two-session day for pupils and teachers would also have to be carefully considered.

Many schools have regular meetings of parents in order to consider educational issues. Here is an opportunity to discuss, perhaps, what parents can do to help children's education, and a tactful headteacher could lead the discussion on why things sometimes go wrong for a child when home and school have different ideals. Advisers and inspectors now play a part in this work, talking to groups of parents and planning, with the headteacher, sessions on various aspects of the school's curriculum and policy. These occasions can become less formal than the lecture situation, and workshops can be set up so that parents themselves handle the new mathematics equipment, for example, and learn some of the language of modern education. One occasion when parents and teachers can come together is Christmas, when they could help to organize the school's celebration. Christmas is a time too when parents can be advised about presents for children, especially where buying books is concerned. Some schools now have an annual book exhibition in November, showing parents what are good books for children of different ages, and warning them against the rubbish which they may otherwise be persuaded to buy.

Planning parental involvement in a new school
Many old schools have done excellent work and have gained the full support of the parents. But the building of a new replacement school can cause great consternation when the parents hear of its open plan design, and a wise headteacher will prepare the community for its new school long before the old building is vacated.

In the first place, it is essential to win the support of school managers. Often local education officers and advisers will gladly accept invitations from a management committee to explain the design of the school, and its possible advantages. The managers should be kept informed of the building project and their cooperation could be sought by inviting them to meetings with architects and other officials of the authority. Any difficulties which might arise could be discussed by organizing a visit of managers and parents to an established school similar, if possible, to the proposed replacement school. The opinions of a staff already operating an open plan organization will often help worried managers and parents.

Enterprising headteachers have been known to seek the cooperation of a local newspaper. Articles and photographs of the new school are printed in the newspaper, and the headteacher has the chance to put across his point of view to the community. Developing from this, schools could prepare little guides to the old and the proposed new school, explaining the differences and helping parents to understand some of the principles involved in planning the new building.

It is becoming a familiar task to advisers and inspectors for them to meet parents, particularly the most critical and vocal ones, in order to give an explanation of what the new building will have to offer children. It seems sensible that officials who advocate opening the teaching spaces in school buildings should be prepared also to support the teachers who have to win the enthusiasm of parents.

Once the new school is in operation, it is still essential to show parents that their children are being cared for and educated properly. The headteacher, no doubt, will invite all the parents to look at the working of the new school as soon as possible. If hundreds of parents are to attend, an after-school function may have to suffice for this. Alternatively, small groups of parents could tour the building in school time, guided by responsible children. The parents could conclude the visit by having a short 'seminar-type' discussion with the head or deputy. Within half a term all parents could have visited in this way, and had frank discussions with the teachers in charge: this is far less worrying to parents who are unwilling to ask questions in a large formal meeting.

One of the best ways of forestalling difficulties from parents is to send home guidebooks on the school. These include short statements about the school and which teachers are responsible for which groups of children. The extracts below are taken from one such guidebook, and it shows how the headteacher has foreseen the parents' worries and put their fears at rest:

> This school is for children between the ages of just under 5 years to 11 years.
>
> There are four infant classes in the department at North Road, and six junior classes in the department at South Street.
>
> The main aim of the school is to provide a happy and secure environment, where children think for themselves and use their own initiative as often as possible. As far as it is possible to sum it up in a few words, we try to teach them how to learn, rather than to drill them with facts.
>
> We invite parents to help us fulfil this aim by mutual exchange of ideas and information. Parents are always welcome here.
>
> Do not be puzzled by anything connected with the school — come and find out!

This is followed by details of hours of attendance, names of staff (teachers, secretary, welfare assistants, meals supervisors, caretaker and crossing patrol officer) and the board of management. There are brief notes on the school curriculum, and parents' anxieties are relieved by such comments as:

Reading
We use the Initial Teaching Alphabet (i.t.a.). All new parents are given a printed book explaining this in detail. It has been in use here for some years and it has proved its worth.

Mathematics
More changes have come about over the last few years in this subject than in any other. The emphasis is now on understanding of mathematical processes, rather than on repetitive learning of half understood facts. This deeper understanding is a much better preparation for work at later stages.

Religious Education
There is a corporate act of worship each day. This is entirely non-denominational. At least one day each week the children conduct their own service.

Remedial Education
Children falling behind with their work are often grouped for special help, especially with reading. In some cases the Educational Psychologist is called in to advise, in which case parents are consulted first.

The Timetable
There is no set timetable, except where certain rooms are needed at certain times. Teachers organize their own day, and work to their own schemes, within a certain agreed framework.

There are notes such as these on French, music, physical education, school visits, medical inspections, school meals, clothing (there is no school uniform 'because the children are so well dressed and colourful that it would seem a pity to lose this variety. However, most of us would agree perhaps on what is sensible for school wear . . .'), care of children (parents are asked to see that children cross the busy road at the crossing patrol, etc), the visits of students ('From time to time students work in the school: children's work is not allowed to suffer, and usually there is some benefit from a fresh approach, and the fact that the teacher can give a little extra time to children who need it'). The booklet finishes with:

If anything in this booklet is not clear, or if further explanation is required, please come. We should like to feel that we are in the same team as you, doing the best possible for the children.

It is perhaps not surprising that the school sending this booklet out to homes does not have complaints from parents. Education officers spend a great deal of time investigating parental complaints and worries, and they would have occasion to thank any school which sets out to work with parents as the compilers of this booklet have done. It is not necessary that the school's guidebook should be a glossy, lavish affair that some PTAs in the United States produce. Simple, welcoming and informative guides to the school can be easily prepared on stencils, and they can go a long way to gain the support and interest of parents.

The school's relationships with the local community can be a two-way process. While parents come into the school, children can go out to help where possible: this is now a normal enough development in secondary schools, but there is no reason why the younger children should not make a contribution. Some schools organize gifts for the old people of the community (usually in connection with the harvest festival), and sometimes children give concerts and musical entertainments in community centres.

There is a growing recognition that the school curriculum should make provision for even the youngest pupils to gain an awareness of a community. Environmental studies, which has replaced such subjects as history, geography and science in many infant and junior schools, is being widened in scope to include far more on the social life of a community. Environmental and social studies should help children to appreciate their own involvement in a community, and they should have the chance to learn how each individual has a contribution to make. The broad aims could be included in a school's schemes of work for the whole age range. Thus the youngest infants could work on a theme such as 'Me' or 'Myself', starting from their own names, ages and birthdays, and going on to learn about relations, friends and pets. Their own interests and needs — toys, games, food, clothing, bodies etc — could all be discussed and made the basis for work. Older infants could then extend the study from their own immediate interests, and think about their 'Homes'. Such a topic would cover the home , its rooms, people who live there and people who visit them (postmen, milkmen, relations, friends), what houses are built of, things which grow in the garden, homes in winter and summer, and so on. The circle is widened later when the theme becomes 'Roundabout my Home', where the children, by making walks around the school with their teacher, learn about their environment, and study the roads and streets, the shopping centres, the churches, doctors, bus stops and routes, garages (where Daddy buys his petrol), the journeys to school, the parks and other spaces near to home. Another theme could be 'My School', with children learning about teachers, friends, classrooms (plans of school spaces), services (school meals, library, coal, milk, biscuits, water, gas, electricity), the school nurse, the secretary, the work of the caretaker and so on. Juniors could extend all these topics, paying, perhaps, special attention to the mapwork involved, and learning more about the relationships between the environment and the lives of the people who live in it. Local services (shopkeepers, doctors, builders, librarians etc) and their distribution will help young children to appreciate the complex social demands involved in the life of a community. They should also have an opportunity to study the changing community, so that they can realize the effect of the passing of time upon people's ways of life. Much worthwhile history can begin with the study of an old school logbook (the children compare their school today with that of children in 1870 — the clothes they wore, their illnesses, the subjects they studied, how they went to work part-time in factories – all these topics and many more are recorded in school logbooks).

Relationships between schools

It is a fact that in many areas the barriers between parents and teachers are falling, but unfortunately the barriers between one school and another are as immovable as they ever were. Primary education should be a totality, and the work of infant and junior schools or departments should dovetail. All too often, junior schools appear ignorant of the work of infant schools while infant teachers may well, as pioneers (and sometimes the unnecessary guardians) of modern methods, suspect the aims and approaches of junior school teachers. Sometimes the lack of communication can reach ridiculous proportions. In one building which housed an infant school on the ground floor and a junior school (different headteacher) above, there was not even discussion about the basic curriculum: at one stage the infants were using metric lengths in mathematics, while the juniors were working in imperial measurement. There was no discussion between the staffs, and it was hardly surprising that the infant children were bewildered by a new way of measuring when they went up to the juniors.

If there are separate infant and junior schools, it is of great importance that teachers from both should meet regularly to discuss the children and the curriculum. They could devise ways of easing the children's transfer from one school to another, and they could consider carefully all the possible causes of children's bewilderment when changing schools. There could be consultation about reading methods, and perhaps infants could take their own familiar reading scheme up with them to the juniors. There could be a common policy about the style of handwriting to be taught, and the basis of the mathematics syllabuses. The advent of 'Fletcher Mathematics', or any other new mathematics scheme, should be carefully considered by both staffs. Fletcher's ideas, for example, need to be introduced at infant level and not with juniors in the first instance.

One way of encouraging cooperation between infant and junior schools or departments is to have an interchange of staff. Many young men teachers in junior schools could be encouraged to spend afternoons with infants, on an exchange basis, and infant teachers could follow up the work of their former pupils by seeing their development as juniors. In primary schools, far more men than women seek promotion to headships, and it is very desirable that future headmasters of junior, mixed and infant schools should be familiar with infant work. Ideally, headteachers should be expert in both infant and junior work but, alas, few short lists of applicants contain candidates who have worked with children right through the age range of five to eleven.

There should not be a great difference between the methodology of the infant school and that of the juniors. There will be certain differences connected with the interests of older juniors and those of infants, and children's spans of concentration will differ, but on the whole the work of infant teachers, with their emphasis on children's all-round development as individuals, should be continued into the junior and even into the secondary schools.

The gulf between primary and secondary schools remains a very wide one. It is not easy for subject specialist teachers of secondary schools to understand the life of a general-purposes class teacher in a primary school. And yet there must be a growth in understanding from both sides if children are to benefit. There is a great deal that needs to be considered by primary and secondary teachers working together. The curricula of both kinds of schools need to be considered simply to remove the many anomalies that now exist. It is possible now to go into neighbouring primary and secondary schools and find wide differences in such basic things as the mathematics syllabuses – one kind of school may be using modern mathematics while others are using traditional syllabuses. Again, modern foreign languages are taught in some primary schools, and not in others, yet the secondary school receives pupils from both kinds of school. Many children, too, are bored to tears when the secondary history syllabus begins again with stone-age man and two years are then spent galloping through the centuries to reach 1485 by the end of the second year.

One possible solution to many problems of this nature is for every secondary school to set up with its feeder primary schools a structure of standing working parties, whose duties would be the consideration of various aspects of the curriculum. This should be connected with visits of teachers to each other's schools, and even to some exchange of teachers. There are certain aspects of the curriculum – music, for example – where the secondary specialist and the primary school class teachers could work together in an area. Authorities could even appoint certain teachers who could work in both kinds of schools as a normal part of their contract.

The growth of the larger secondary schools has frequently led to the appointment of first year tutors or lower school heads, and these senior posts carry responsibility for liaising with primary schools in an area. These are very worthwhile duties, and they could be extended by enlisting the secondary heads of departments in the work of liaising with the subject enthusiasts in the primary schools. Ideally, each area should have its own mathematics, remedial, social studies, music, etc working parties, reporting to primary headteachers and to the lower school tutors in charge.

Conclusion
Much that has been said in this chapter is about personal relationships. It could well be argued that our educational system has been blunting people's capacity for deep, loving relationships. Society's emphasis is increasingly on success and the pursuit of one's own happiness. But the essential task for educators is to promote the child's own unselfish self-respect and sensitivity to others. Sometimes we, as teachers, become so involved in academic prowess, in organizing, testing and grading

children (some are labelled 'slow learners' or 'remedials'; a better adjective would be 'libelled'), that we forget that a more fundamental duty is to encourage the uniqueness of every child and to help him develop genuine, worthwhile relationships with the people about him. Many different people contribute to the child's growth in the community — parents, teachers in primary and secondary schools, school managers and governors, workers in the community, ancillary workers in the school, and many others. All of them can work together for the common good of the children and their open plan primary school. A great deal will depend upon the wisdom and example of the headteacher. It is for him to establish a happy, industrious school of high standards through the appointment of a staff who can work together, and through his success in making his school 'open' in the sense that it becomes a thriving and welcoming part of the community.

References
DOUGLAS, J. W. B. (1964) *The Home and the School* London: Mac-Gibbon and Kee

Further reading

ALLEN, D. (Ed) (1973) *Early Years at School* London: BBC

BREARLEY, M. (Ed) (1970) *Fundamentals in the First School* London: Blackwell

BROWN, M. and PRECIOUS, N. (1968) *The Integrated Day in the Primary School* London: Ward Lock Educational

DES (1967) *Children and their Primary Schools* (Plowden Report) London: HMSO

DES (1972) *Open Plan Primary Schools* (Education Survey No. 16) London: HMSO

FOSTER, J. (1971) *Recording Individual Progress* (Basic Books in Education Series) London: Macmillan

GARDNER, D. E. M. (1966) *Experiment and Tradition in Primary Schools* London: Methuen

KOHL, H. (1970) *The Open Classroom* London: Methuen

MATHEMATICAL ASSOCIATION (1970) *Primary Mathematics – a further report* London: Bell

PALMER, R. (1972) *Space, Time and Grouping* (British Primary Schools Today Series) London: Macmillan

PEARSON, E. (1972) *Trends in School Design* (British Primary Schools Today Series) London: Macmillan

RANCE, P. (1971) *Record Keeping in the Progressive Primary School* London: Ward Lock Educational

RIDGWAY, L. and LAWTON, I. (1965) *Family Grouping in the Primary School* London: Ward Lock Educational

SCHOOLS COUNCIL (1965) *Mathematics in Primary Schools* London: HMSO

TAYLOR, J. (1971) *Organizing and Integrating the Infant Day* London: Allen and Unwin

Index